Kinoti's conflict transformatic [experiences, offering a hands-on approach that releases you to experience joy, freedom, and authentic relationships. It's a must-read for frontline practitioners involved in peace and development as well as for marketplace leaders who are confronted with conflicts each day of their lives!

—**Dr Daniel Muvengi, Africa Director for Faith & Development Programming, World Vision East Africa**

This upbeat volume is a must-read for peacemakers in Africa. In its manageable dimensions, Kinoti nevertheless sets forth decades of experience in peacemaking in 15 countries, offering timeless wisdom relevant for individuals, families, churches, estranged couples, pastors, counsellors, business and political leaders, and company CEOs.

Via multiple case studies, Kinoti shows how conflict is both normal and inevitable, but its forces can be harnessed to become constructive rather than destructive, healing rather than lethal. This is the genius of the volume. I cannot recommend it highly enough.

—**Michael Cassidy, Founder of African Enterprise, South Africa**

At a time when conflicts abound at almost every level, this book is a gift. It is wonderfully clear and surprisingly simple, in the sense of being readable. Yet it is full of deep wisdom plus very practical tools for all of us. Consider reading it yourself and recommending it to anyone who wants help with a conflict.

—**Jane Overstreet, President of Development Associates International, USA**

Among books written on conflict resolution, *Making Peace with Fire* is uniquely grounded in biblical teaching. I encourage everybody regardless of religion or race to read it. You will get skills to create peaceful relationships in your family and society.

—**Rev Dr Abdi Tadesse, Christian-Muslim Relations Program Coordinator at Mekane Yesus Seminary, Ethiopia**

You will benefit immensely from the content of this book. Using his personal experiences and expertise as a teacher, Kinoti captures the transformative power of conflict when channelled properly. This book is packed with information and strategies that will help you see conflict in a new light, and develop the skills needed to strengthen and keep your valuable relationships. It is incisive, simple to understand, and timely.

Written from a Christian perspective, the book's wisdom will enrich anyone regardless of their religion: leaders, pastors, teachers, followers, and all who desire to see a better world. This is a book that should be on everyone's bookshelf. Don't just wish for peace, work for it as a peace advocate. As more people learn conflict transformation skills, our families and societies will enjoy the fruits of peace.

—Rev Dr Gideon Para-Mallam, President and CEO, The Para-Mallam Peace Foundation, Nigeria

Kinoti has clearly and beautifully provided practical skills and competencies to guide towards handling conflict productively. This is an effective tool not only for individuals and families, but also for relational living environments where other relationships flourish. I recommend this book to everyone who is involved in peacebuilding on both personal and communal level. These principles are foundations for living in the community without regrets.

—Rev Dr Célestin Musekura, Founder & President, ALARM US

Making Peace with Fire is more than just an added resource in the myriad of books on the subject of forgiveness or reconciliation. Kinoti takes us a step further to conflict transformation! Writing with a vast array of experience – from a rural Kenyan tribe to an international education to experience in global consulting – he takes us through the process of turning the fires of conflict into the warm respect of fruitful and deep friendships. If you've ever experienced conflict – which is all of us – you need this book!

—Dr Paul Borthwick, Missionary with Development Associates International, Author of *Western Christians in Global Mission* and *Great Commission, Great Compassion*, USA

Conflict is inevitable in a world filled with difference. Every leader should ask, "How can we engage in conflict in such a way that difference does not invite destruction?" Thankfully, Kinoti teaches leaders to move conflict from a destructive to a constructive force. Kinoti weaves together theory and practice in a digestible and actionable fashion for leaders serving in this world of difference. It is worth the read, but even more worth putting into practice.

—**Dr John Thexton, Sr. Director of Community Life,
Denver Rescue Mission, USA**

Kinoti gives readers priceless nuts and bolts for conflict transformation he has developed through his life experiences. Without a doubt, this book is invaluable for anyone engaged in the work of peace building and conflict.

—**Dr Helen Nambalirwa Nkabala, Director of Rotary Peace Center
and Associate Professor of Religion and Peace Studies
at Makerere University, Kampala, Uganda**

In a world where volatile rhetoric is lauded as smart clickbait and power brokers leverage "us versus them" dichotomies to advance their agendas, Kinoti presents a much-needed alternate faith-driven reality. Instead of conflict for manipulation, this book offers a better way: conflict that beautifully transforms into growth opportunities.

Through foundational best practices and experiential tenets of leadership, spirituality, and psychology, Kinoti offers a path for relational healing and conflict resolution. As a Christian and an expert in the psychology of human relationships, I'm grateful for this practical and credible tool.

—**Dr Harold L. Arnold, Jr., author of *The Unfair Advantage:
A grace-inspired path to winning at marriage*, USA**

Timely, thought-provoking, easy-to-read, and well-articulated research. This book is full of practical experience and solution-based principles for resolving conflicts in any context you may find yourself. I strongly recommend it for every organization and individual who desires growth in human relationships and productivity!

—**Rev Johnson O. Okoroafor, CEO of Touchstone Ministries
International and Senior Pastor of Touchstone Mission
Baptist Church, Yaoundé, Cameroon**

As a psychotherapist and family mediator, I can attest that interpersonal conflicts are on the rise. *Making Peace with Fire* is a timely resource. Kinoti, as a Christian and global professional in peace-building, retools the best of us with knowledge and skills to understand and handle conflict. The book's experiential insights and biblical principles empower you to look at conflict's constructive and destructive potential. I recommend this book as one of the best guides for humans from all walks of life to transform conflicts into stronger relationships.

—**Dr Charity Waithima, Assistant Professor of Psychology at United States International University Africa and Mental Health Consultant, Kenya**

Kinoti provides real-life experiences and the Word of God as a clear guide to resolving conflicts of every kind. His principles will help many people to untie themselves from the high costs of conflicts. Because of its interactive nature, I highly recommend this book for study by individuals, groups, and institutions.

—**Rev Justus Mugambi, Deputy Bishop, Christ is the Answer Ministries (CITAM), Kenya**

Illuminating . . . An excellent exposition and training manual in peace and conflict transformation, whether for individuals, academia, NGOs, or churches. Kinoti holistically integrates appropriate cultural and biblical situations. His expert use of case studies, relevant everyday illustrations, and guiding questions in each chapter make this book highly practical for those involved in hands-on conflict transformation work.

—**Beatrice Ndirangu, Conflict Transformation Expert and Businesswoman, Kenya**

M.D. KINOTI, PhD

Making Peace
FIGHTING FIRE
WITH FIRE

Harnessing conflict to
transform your relationships

OASIS
INTERNATIONAL
PUBLISHING

ISBN 13: 978-1-59452-867-5
ISBN: 1-59452- 867-5

Published by Oasis International Ltd.

**Oasis International is a ministry devoted to growing discipleship through publishing
African voices.**
- We *engage* Africa's most influential, most relevant, and best communicators for the sake
  of the gospel.
- We *cultivate* local and global partnerships in order to publish and distribute high-quality
  books and Bibles.
- We *create* contextual content that meets the specific needs of Africa, has the power to
  transform individuals and societies, and gives the church in Africa a global voice.
Oasis is: *Satisfying Africa's Thirst for God's Word.*
For more information, go to oasisinternational.com.

Cover design: Bupe Katungwa | Interior design: Natascha Olivier, Coco Design

Printed in India.

23 24 25 26 27 28 29 30 31 32 BPI 10 9 8 7 6 5 4 3 2 1

Making Peace with Fire

Table of Contents

1

Why Conflict Transformation Matters

> "Never pay back evil with more evil. Do things in such a way that everyone can see you are honourable. *Do all that you can* to live in peace with everyone."
>
> (ROMANS 12:17-18, ITALICS MINE)

If you are reading this book, I am guessing you don't like conflict. Perhaps you are hoping that this book will help you avoid conflict. I, too, have had more than enough conflict in my life.

I was born in a rural community in northeastern Kenya in what many would consider a dysfunctional family – which is a good descriptor for most families anyway! Being a polygamous family introduced a unique layer of conflict among my father's three wives and over 15 children. Many of these have carried on to our adult lives.

We also had conflicts with neighbours, the clan, and neighbouring tribes, the Somali and the Dorobo. As young kids in the 1970s, we would be taught how to run and hide in the bushes when we heard gunshots because that would mean we were under attack by the *shiftas*, Somali raiders. Thankfully, the *shiftas* never made it to our home village. Still, stories persisted of nearby communities that faced attacks until what was considered the complete eradication of these terrorist groups in the early 1980s.

My extended family and my clan considered it their duty to train me to perpetuate generations-old conflicts. This was, of course, all done with the best intentions. When I was about 15, our large clan organized three meetings for me and more than 20 of my cousins to be educated in the ways of our ancestors. At our grandfather's home, we were schooled on our history, where our ancestors came from, whom we could marry and not marry because of good or bad family relations and myths, and above all, who our enemies were. It was a shocking realization that one of my best friends in school came from a clan that "we were not supposed to have any dealings with". His clan also held similar meetings and they were given identical instructions. Of course, this confused us all and left our relationships in shambles.

When I went to university, I was one of the Christian Union leaders on campus. Members from some of the tribes decided to split off and create their own tribal-based fellowships separate from the main Christian Union group. We painfully tried to work through our differences, but without success. The church I joined after graduation also went through a mean-spirited conflict and a messy break-up. I felt confused and sad that our leaders, Christians, could not address their differences. When I got a job at an international Christian organization, I was shocked to find exactly the same power plays, gossip, and fights over interests, personalities, and resources I would have expected only in a secular organization.

Later, in marriage, in my family, and in immigrating from Kenya to the United States, I found conflict at every turn. Conflict seemed to be a theme in my life! I couldn't escape it, so I realized I needed to learn how to transform conflict into something positive. Studying conflicts and how to transform them made an important difference to my own life and the lives of others as I began to practise and teach the skills for conflict transformation. In this book, I offer the insights I have gathered from experience, training, and in my practice as a mediator and professor, to help you in your quest to understand your own conflicts and transform your relationships.

Conflicts Are Costly

We don't usually have positive associations with conflict – and for a good reason!

Conflicts are painful. They often bring out the worst in us and others. Sharp words, insults, accusations, cruel actions, or stonewalling are painful. They can cause deep emotional wounds. We feel angry because our expectations, values, or goals are being challenged. Our insecurities are often attacked, leaving us feeling vulnerable. Perhaps we feel ashamed of how we acted or feel sad, grieving the loss of valuable relationships.

There is a cost to conflict, especially when it comes to relationships. Trust is eroded, and that trust may be difficult – or take a long time – to rebuild. Relationships change and sometimes end. People in conflict are also likely to fear "losing face" among other relations (for example, family, colleagues, and community members). When word spreads in an office or a community that someone is often involved in fights, they may lose other relationships as people take sides or distance themselves. Worse still is if the escalating conflict involves several family members, teams, or communities, disrupting the harmony in relationships.

Conflicts can be costly if they are poorly managed. This is especially true when we react negatively and the conflict then escalates. A disagreement on an office project may, for example, deteriorate into non-cooperation or, worse, shouting at each other.

Time and effort are wasted as the conflict takes centre stage instead of focusing on the work. As a result, the conflict leads to reduced performance, missed deadlines, or poor work. Emotional distress rises, so people withdraw from others or stall on tasks. Perhaps they even skip coming into the office in order to avoid the people who offended them. Eventually, the stress may lead to mental health or other health issues, resulting in even further loss of productivity.

Escalating conflicts can lead to the breakdown of relationships and result in expensive court cases. They can also lead to other significant financial losses, such as opportunity costs, break-up costs, etc. If violence is involved, there are medical and legal bills.

We Can't Avoid Conflict

Conflict is a normal part of life. To be human and to be in a relationship with others is to experience conflict. I know that sounds gloomy, but it is the truth. If you are lucky, the conflicts are few, and the episodes are not severe enough to break up a relationship. Many of us, however, have been involved in conflicts that have escalated and led to a breakdown in our relationships. Because we need social interaction, we need to accept that we will have conflict, otherwise we will get highly frustrated with relationships. Conflict is simply what happens when you have relationships, expectations, and differences.

Relationships

Although we may sometimes describe contradictory ideas or opinions in our minds as conflicts ("Should I eat this or that meal?"), actual conflicts are about relationships with other people.

We all live in a web of relationships. Some of these relationships are direct, such as a family member (spouse, father or grandchild, for example), while others are indirect or extended, such as with a friend of my neighbour or my boss's child. We constantly relate with others at home, school, or at work as we go about our days. The closer the relationship, the more possibilities for direct conflict.

For instance, we all know families who are plagued by conflict. Perhaps they squabble over ownership of the family property or resources like water or grazing land. If the family members were not in a relationship with each other, there would be no reason for these conflicts.

Other relationships can also be clearly broken, and then escalate, sometimes even to violence. In my birth district, a worker attacked and killed an employer because of a disagreement over payment. This was extremely tragic on so many levels. No amount of disagreement should lead to the death of another person.

However, it later emerged that the employer had been mistreating his workers for a while. He would employ them on his tea farm and not pay them on time. He would demand a lot from them and deduct their pay for even the least of infractions, like picking fruit from his farm. Because he was well connected with the police and those in power, he would come up with false accusations and have some of his workers arrested just to intimidate them.

One worker was so deeply riled over being mistreated that he took matters into his hands, attacking his employer with a machete, killing him. This was, of course, a heinous crime that landed the employee in prison for life. But the two were in conflict because they were in a broken relationship.

We shouldn't get rid of conflict by simply getting rid of relationships. As humans, we are created to need other people. We are made for and thrive in our connection with others. Children are born dependent on care from their parents in ways that many newborn animals do not need. Research shows that humans will wither and die if they are removed from others.

It is not good for humans to be alone, God said in the beginning. So God created man and woman and, by extension, all humans to live in relationships with one another, with God, and with the rest of creation (Genesis 2:18). Unfortunately, by disobeying God, all those relationships fell apart, landing the first humans and their children in messed-up relations, which we have been trying to mend ever since. But the truth is that it is still not good for us to be alone.

Expectations

Relationships develop over time. As we engage with another person, we also start to form expectations. Consciously or subconsciously, we place specific demands on our interactions with others. We all come to relationships with a set of expectations, often for what that relationship should be, what it will deliver, and how we will be better off because we are in it. In committed long-term relationships like marriage, many soon discover that they expect a lot from their spouses. These may not be based on who their spouse is, but rather on how they saw their parents interact or the ways they related within their families of origin. Even when you work at an office, you bring a particular set of expectations. An employer, colleagues, and clients also have expectations of a new employee, for example.

Expectations may vary, depending on the type of relationship. They may be communicated, like in a job description, or learned along the way, as in a family. Some are instilled in us as we grow up and are therefore held subconsciously. Some are learned from observing families and communities. When in a relationship with another person, we expect particular treatment – in words, deeds, and responses. We are frustrated when these are missing or different from what we expected. For instance, my wife and children get frustrated when I project onto them the same high expectations, I have for myself – especially when they don't see the issue the way I do!

> ⑦ Think about a conflict you had. Which relationships were affected by the conflict? Which expectations impacted the conflict? Which differences were involved in the conflict?
>
> ....
> ....
> ....
> ....

Unrealistic expectations quickly lead us into conflict. For example, expecting a family member always to relate kindly and respectfully is unrealistic. If we demand this, the moment the other person misses the mark, there will certainly be conflict. However, even realistic expectations can result in conflict, simply because they place demands on someone who may not be able to meet them.

Still, expectations are inevitable because they set the purpose of the relationship and provide a guide for meaningful interactions with others. We can't, therefore, avoid conflict by avoiding expectations.

Differences

Conflict often arises from our differences. If we engage with other people, we will soon find that, just as we are different in our physical make-up, we will also have differences in how we see things and approach situations. Our unique perspectives, personalities, and experiences often mean differing opinions, actions, and potential disagreements. If these are not handled correctly, they may escalate into conflict.

For example, I am an extrovert, while my late wife was an introvert. If we went out to a party, I would be all over the place, trying to meet as many people as possible. She would identify one or two individuals she felt comfortable with, usually fellow introverts, and spend the rest of the party chatting with them. As a result, at the end of the evening, I would bring home a stack of business cards, while she would bring a deeper knowledge of her friends.

Unfortunately, these personality differences could cause friction. I would often push my wife to "get out of the house" while she would pull me "back home". In conversations with other people, I often processed stuff "out there" and wished she would speak up more, while she would be quiet and comment only if pushed to do so, sometimes feeling that I had said too much.

The solution to avoiding conflict is not to minimize or erase our differences. Differences are often natural and good. For example, in family and work relationships, having different opinions on whether or not to take a specific action is not bad. Differences are to be expected when more than one person considers an issue. Different views and opinions can enrich the experience of working or living together. Someone in the team or family may have information about the issue that others do not have. Someone else might have made a similar decision in another context and seen the results. Or, in deliberations, new wisdom might arise to help the team make a more informed decision. The results of considering different opinions can be positive.

Conflict Is Like Fire

If we accept that conflict is an unavoidable part of living in a relationship with other people, we will come to realize that our goal can't be to avoid conflict. Instead, we need to develop skills to responsibly handle whatever expectations and differences arise in our relationships with care. We also need to bring our expectations in line with reality.

The Swahili have a saying, "*dawa ya moto ni moto*" – literally, "the medicine for fire is fire". Meaning that you need to fight fire with fire. Unfortunately, I have never heard this saying used in any constructive context. Instead, it is often used to argue that you should approach contentious situations with more, rather than less aggression. Attack those who attack you with as much force as they applied. But tit-for-tat or revenge approaches tend to feed fires with more fuel. When you light a fire to quell another fire, you can imagine the destruction that follows.

Sometimes, conflict feels like a volcano that will inevitably erupt or a fire raging uncontrollably across the grasslands. We think we can do nothing but watch the situation explode and destroy our homes and livelihoods. Our emotions feel like they are bubbling up under the surface, and all we can do is try to rein them in. It is true that handling conflicts carelessly or ignoring them can escalate tension, which can eventually destroy lives, families, and communities – even nations! That is why many books and materials advocate for conflict resolution or conflict management. Their approach is to quash conflicts because they are considered negative. The view is that this will bring about peace between individuals. This short-term thinking rarely takes the value of building relationships seriously.

I argue that conflict is like a fire. Yes, it has the potential for destruction if it is not managed well. If we add fuel to the fire, even a small fire will grow and can become dangerous. How we react to these regular occurrences can determine whether differences will escalate to more resounding opposition.

But if we can keep it from escalating, fire does not just destroy. It can create new things. Fire starts engines and takes us to new places, just as conflict can take us in new directions. Fire transforms dough into bread and raw meat into a delicious meal; in the same way, conflict often transforms us and our relationships into something new. You learn how to relate to the other person differently, or you figure out a tactic to address the issues that divide you. Fire also keeps us warm; when there is no conflict in a relationship, that may be a sign of cold distance that could lead to the end of a relationship. Since we tend to argue with those closest to us, knowing how to do this in ways that preserve the relationships is not only a valuable gift in transforming these crucial bonds, but will also bring joy to our lives when we are able to strengthen rather than throw away these essential connections.

Fire purifies metals too. Disagreements help us to clarify the goal of our interactions or endeavours. We often assume that everyone has the same goals – until we disagree. Conflict gives us the reality check to clear up unhealthy perceptions and refocus the relationship. Taking the time to communicate our expectations helps to determine the next steps in the undertaking – including walking away from each other if necessary. Disagreements force us to re-evaluate issues and often offer problem-solving opportunities.

That is why this book focuses on conflict transformation. Accepting that conflict is necessary and normal, we build on proven approaches to handling conflict to safeguard relationships. Differences and even conflicts can be constructive, not just destructive. That is why, even though this book is about conflict, it is both upbeat and positive. The skills you develop here could save and strengthen your relationships now and in the future. As more people learn to address root causes, the more we will cement the bonds that keep our relationships peaceful in families, workplaces, and societies. The more we understand conflict transformation, the better our cooperative lives and world will be.

For those of you reading this to develop leadership skills, I commend you because successful leadership includes harnessing the power of dissent and different opinions. Influential leaders

leadership

invite and intentionally manage conflicts. A company or organization with conflict may mean team members with differing ideas feel comfortable contributing them. They are not ignored or silenced, so the vision of the place is not dulled. Leaders who thoughtfully and carefully invite alternative views are providing the fertilizer for growth. A healthy exchange of ideas in open and constructive discussions has the potential for discovering hidden gems, better ideas, and creative solutions.

In all our relationships, if we have a healthy appreciation of conflicts and the skills to confront these situations effectively, we can harness the fire and healthily engage the other party. This can transform many conflicts into opportunities to learn, grow, expand our perspectives, preserve relationships, and make better choices.

From Scared to Prepared

So why do we react to conflicts as though they are volcanos or raging fires in the wild savannah grasslands? We are often scared of conflict because we are unprepared. Unable to direct and use the fire, we feel out of control and fear the worst. The possibility of an emotional confrontation with another person can be terrifying, even to the most courageous of us. We don't know what to do. Some of us freeze or walk away disgustedly, blaming the other party for the misunderstanding.

Given how conflict is so much a part of our daily lives, you would expect us to be experts in handling conflict. You would think we would have a ton of courses and training on how to handle conflict in healthy ways. But scan any school curriculum or degree programme, and you will be lucky to find a course focusing on this critical aspect of our human reality. Even in our leadership and management development programmes, we don't spend enough time on conflict. We do, however, know that management is a process of dealing with people, which therefore means dealing with differing ideas, personalities, and conflicts.

If you are like me, how you were brought up may not have helped. Many families and communities do not model the best ways to resolve differences or carefully work through issues with love and respect. No wonder we need more preparation on what to do when we step into spaces where we encounter differences. As a result, our workplaces, families, social spaces, places of worship, and community gatherings are prone to disruption from even the simplest disagreements. We dislike conflicts because we don't know how to handle them well.

That is how I felt when confronted with all the ethnic, family, workplace, and church conflicts I encountered. Being a well-meaning global citizen, I decided to study human conflicts. I believed there must be a better way to handle conflict than just exploding. When it came to conflict and peacebuilding, I thought that, as Christians, our faith must have something to offer us. And, indeed, Christians do have something better to offer the world.

My research did not disappoint. I learned that the Bible is full of stories and teachings that call us to be peacemakers. What's more, I began to discover principles that worked. A few years after getting

How do you and your family relate with each other when in conflict? How does this affect how you deal with conflicts with other people beyond your family?

. . . .

. . . .

. . . .

. . . .

my PhD in interethnic peacebuilding, I also trained as a cross-cultural mediator. I have spent the last two decades teaching peacebuilding and interpersonal relations, teaching the leaders of non-profit organizations and churches at Regis University in the US and more than 15 countries worldwide. I have also consulted international NGOs on team dynamics and cross-cultural skills development. I am honoured that Development Associates International invited me to develop a conflict transformation course that they now use in over 20 countries for their master's programme.

Having worked most of my life to understand and address the issues that divide us, I still hope we can learn to live at peace with one another. Conflicts and hatred are learned, and we can intentionally learn to reverse these ideas and grow in peace and understanding.

What to Expect in This Book

This book will help you grow in conflict competence so you can be prepared for conflict. Conflict competence is the personal awareness and ability to positively engage in conflict through collaborative means that reduce conflict escalation and possible harm. You can develop constructive mental, emotional, and behavioural skills to address conflict. These skills include the ability to:

- control emotional reactions that could escalate the conflict,
- step back and analyse the causes of the conflict,
- accept and admit personal responsibility for the conflict where necessary,
- separate the issues from the person,
- overcome tendencies that stall transformation, including a temptation to "fight or flight",
- map out possible solutions for managing and transforming the situation,

- develop trust and the safety measures necessary to address the conflict, and
- learn from the case for future engagements.

Developing conflict competence is a long process that requires practice. You will not be able to do all the above on your first major conflict, but they remain crucial skills that will help ensure that significant relationships thrive.

Since I have written this book from a Christian perspective, I ground most of the material in biblical teachings. I believe the Bible contains essential guidelines for positive living, principles, and lessons that teach us a positive approach to not only our relationships with others but also to conflict. Some of my favourite teachings about peacemaking come from the Bible: "God blesses those who work for peace, for they will be called the children of God" (Matthew 5:9). The Bible calls Christians to live at peace with others, to the extent that it depends on them (Romans 12:18). This includes doing good (Psalm 34:14) and pursuing what leads to the benefit of others (Romans 14:19).

That does not mean that this book is written for Christians only. Indeed, the information contained here is valid for everyone, religious or not. Through my learning, I have distilled practical principles that I will share to help you harness the power of conflict to transform your relationships. Anyone can learn these conflict principles to make our world a better place.

A better understanding of ourselves and our conflicts is part of healthy human development. I use stories and case studies from actual and could-be-true stories to illustrate those principles. I also include diagrams, drawings, and quotes, all carefully selected to emphasize a point for your consideration and further discussion.

Reaction boxes are good spaces to jot down ideas, respond to questions, and prepare responses for action. Whatever you do, do not skip these! They are important in your learning process. I invite you to evaluate and reflect on the conflicts in your life as you work through the book. You will be grateful you did.

I have also included study questions at the end of each chapter so that you can engage others around you in reviewing your thinking. Invite them to read and discuss these ideas with you by organizing a study group. Learning in community is the best way of expanding our knowledge and helps break down the barriers to speaking about conflicts. Reading the book is essential, but your own processing of the content will ultimately be more beneficial. I hope this book becomes more like a personal journal you can refer to often.

I pray that this book helps you become a peacebuilder in your relationships. Committing to peace is the first step towards developing societies devoted to a culture of peace.

Think back to what you learned about conflict as you were growing up. It could be from interactions with family or colleagues or formal courses, seminars, or workshops. If you could summarize some of the lessons they taught you about conflict in brief taglines, what would they be? List them here.

- ....
  ....
- ....
  ....
- ....
  ....
- ....
  ....
- ....
  ....

Group Discussion

1. What are some of the benefits you have seen from conflict? What are some of the costs of conflict you have seen in your relationships?

2. Discuss the metaphor of fire for conflict. How does thinking about the uses of fire and its dangers affect your thinking about conflicts in your life or in others' lives?

How Did We Get Here?

> ## Vita, vita vitapata (SWAHILI, EAST AFRICA).
> "War only begets war."
> **MEANING:**
> Unless there is work towards peace,
> all you can expect is more conflict.

To save money, Mana shared a one-room "servants' quarter" with Jimna, someone he had met in university. One day, Mana's distant cousin Kula showed up to stay with them. After graduating from university, Kula had moved to the city to find a job. Mana was supportive and even introduced Kula to some friends who worked at several companies. However, the economy being as tight as it was, Kula struggled to find a job and had remained unemployed for several months.

Jimna was not thrilled when Kula showed up. He had nothing in common with him. Although he was sympathetic to Kula's circumstances, the room they shared was too cramped for three of them. He did not want to move out, partly because he could not afford the rent by himself.

One day after work, Jimna and Mana met at a local coffee shop to talk about Kula's stay. The two had known each other for a few years now. The conversation started respectfully, but the situation turned sour quickly.

Jimna said, "You broke our agreement for renting together. You never told me Kula would be moving in with us. He doesn't pay any bills or even clean up, and it's not like he has something else to do!"

"You think I knew Kula would be moving in? He just showed up at my workplace. But I can't tell my relative he is not welcome. Do you want me to kick him out when I know he has nowhere to go?"

"I don't care, but you must tell him to move out. If you don't, remember that the lease is in my name."

"Seriously? You would toss someone without a job or connections onto the streets? That's inhumane!" Mana started to get emotional, his voice rising.

Jimna started to get agitated. "You think I'm the problem here? Your cousin is the problem. Why are you accusing me?" Soon, the two started shouting at each other. It was no longer a conversation but a full-blown argument.

"This conversation is going nowhere. I'm leaving," said Jimna, as he walked out.

"Where do you think you're going?" called Mana after him.

In the days that followed, whenever Kula walked into the room, Jimna pretended he wasn't there. One day when Kula was out, Jimna gathered all Kula's mess and put it on the couch where Kula slept. When Mana confronted Jimna, he announced he was heading out to meet a friend. "You're not going anywhere," Mana said, and grabbed Jimna's arm. Jimna shoved Mana away, and soon the two were in a fistfight.

Fuelling the Fire

Have you ever found yourself, like Jimna and Kula, wondering how you ended up in a full-blown conflict? Surely just yesterday, it was only a small disagreement!

Remember the most recent conflict you had. What was the first comment or action? What opposing view did the other party offer? Did someone make a harsh comment, or a judgement call on the other party's character or reasoning ability (e.g., "I can't believe you would think like that."). From there, you may have noticed that matters deteriorated quickly. Issues changed or were compounded with every attack or counterattack, to the extent that the original cause was quickly forgotten. Perhaps it became an attack on the person's character, like, "You are so dumb!" Or "This is why my mother warned me not to marry you. She knew men like you do not keep their word." With the fuel of emotional outbursts and character attacks, conflicts tend to grow and become more challenging fires to manage. Even when managed, the relationship will have changed.

We will spend most of this book talking about how to transform conflicts, but first we need to understand how they can spiral out of control. Since our reactions and communication can contribute to escalating conflict, this chapter will also encourage some self-reflection.

Spiralling out of control

The strange thing with conflicts is their potential to grow bigger and worse than expected. If the parties react to the differences in a negative way, emotions are heightened, and the intensity of the differences is magnified. The other party then responds at the same or a slightly higher level with a corresponding reaction, and everything spirals from there.

The situation can then get out of hand. A conflict that grows in intensity can lead to violence – psychological and physical. With every reaction, we dig ourselves into deeper holes until, unfortunately, we cannot dig ourselves out. We damage our relationships. This book will help you learn how to stop conflicts before they lead to violence or damage relationships.

The cause of the conflict is rarely one particular thing, especially in ongoing relationships. When compounded with other ongoing issues, a minor issue becomes a cyclone, gathering strength as it goes. This is called conflict escalation or spiralling.

For instance, the conflict between Jimna and Mana began with them deciding what to do about Kula, but it soon escalated to threats about the lease and Kula's messiness. If the roommates do not resolve the issue quickly, it could grow as other sometimes minor differences, comments, and actions are added. The issues may become unmanageable monsters that consume the roommates' lives and relationships.

The diagram on the next page illustrates how conflicts can grow. The good news is that, with proper management, conflicts can move back towards peace at any point along this spiral.

Conflict usually starts small. Often the parties have different opinions, attitudes, interests, or perceptions of the issues at hand. It could be as mundane as which TV channel to watch, whom to invite to join a committee, or a passing comment in a particular tone of voice. Differences alone do not lead to conflict; everything depends on how we react to them. Some differences might be celebrated or ignored, stopping the spiral.

Differences can, however, lead to disagreement, and when that happens, it is easiest to handle the situation by clarifying any misconceptions you may share. Talk about what each party understood by the situation and realign your shared goals. If the

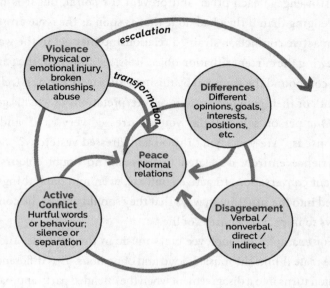

disagreement arose from an action, you could apologize, give restitution, and ensure the injury does not continue. Some people may also stop the conflict by simply burying the issue. Buried issues may well be forgotten, but sometimes, when another issue arises, old hurts are revisited or combined with new hurts, and the reaction may be even more intense.

If the conflict continues, it becomes a tit-for-tat process. There is a common saying in Swahili, "*nipe nikupe*", which means, "Give it to me, and I will give it to you." Or, hit me and I will hit you back. The parties start to blame each other or react in ways that, instead of addressing the core issues that led to the conflict in the first place, add more issues and offences. They may have been hurt by the other party or how that person reacted. They thus end up hurting each other beyond the initial conflict because the matter has now become an emotional one. They are in active conflict. At this step, the parties can still engage each other and prevent the spiral, but it is more challenging than if they had done that as soon as the issue arose.

In active conflicts, a strained relationship may get in the way of reviewing the current situation objectively. Additionally, the parties may compound the situation by raising issues from the past (related or not), or their own perceptions or interpretations of what is going on. One person says, "Today you are dressed very well," and the response is, "Are you saying I was badly dressed yesterday?" Some experience entirely unrelated to dressing no doubt colours the current conversation. In active conflicts, even mundane things get pulled into the situation in ways that they should not, so the conflict grows to impact other areas of life.

For example, an employee plays music in their cubicle, and the office mate thinks the music is loud and obnoxious. This difference in opinion turns into a disagreement when the offended party approaches their colleague. If the music player refuses to change and reacts by playing the music louder, they are in active conflict. The parties may end up piling on other allegations or sabotaging the other's work. Driven by ego and a need to stand their ground, the colleagues damage their relationship.

There is no telling how long the conflict can last or how vicious it can get, especially if the parties insist on their rights and make demands. Soon they feel that they are justified in their attacks on each other. Like locked gears, a conflict can hold parties in a jammed-up position that prevents the relationship from moving forward, instead causing friction and eventually even a break. As the conflict spirals out of control, emotional outbursts, psychological manipulation, and even violence may result. Violence can be any circumstance that destroys a relationship – emotional violence as well as physical assault.

Transformation is nevertheless possible even at the violent stage if the parties are still interested in resolving their issue or if they get help from a third party. However, the deeper they dig into the conflict, the harder it becomes to pull back. It is very difficult because the emotional engagement is now deeper than before. The earlier story of Jimna, Mana, and Kula spun out of control to the point of violence, but it may still be possible to pull back from the brink if both parties can agree to do so. Their relationship may, however, have been changed for good.

Because conflicts are harder to resolve at each step of the spiral, we need to address them as soon as possible.

While this book mostly talks about interpersonal conflict, the conflict spiral can apply to communities as well. Strongly held identities and beliefs about "us" versus "them" can drag us down into hateful ruts, leading to dangerous conflicts and, in extreme instances, even genocide. However, the differences themselves would not necessarily lead to a conflict that spirals out of control. It is the way that people react and escalate the conflict that is the real problem.

Our Reactions

How were you raised to react?

How we behave in relationships, and particularly in the face of conflict, depends largely on habits learned in our development and upbringing. We were all born and trained into ways of thought and behaviour considered appropriate in a particular society. As we observed and practised, we learned cultural values and norms that help us relate to others in our social context. In male, female, children, and adult relationships, we learned how to communicate, argue (or not), and resolve conflict. This programming embeds deep in our being an often unconscious "software" that helps us to operate as humans.

Family and the media play an important role in developing a personal view of self and others. These two forces coach us on how to relate to power, gender differences, expectations, what is most essential for the community and for us, and the appropriate means of achieving personal or group goals (including our desire for comfort). They also help us situate ourselves in relation to other people, especially those outside our cultural groups. Life experiences, education, and exposure not only shape our outlook on life and our relationships with others, but also what we perceive as conflict, how we react in disputes, and understand the dynamics of power.

As a generalization, many Western societies (mainly Europe and North America) emphasize the individual's rights and the individual's place in relation to others and in society in general. A person has the right to engage or disengage with others as they please. If an individual's happiness, comfort, fulfilment, or goals and requests conflict with those of the community, the individual's rights often take precedence. An individual's personal space, emotional boundaries, or limits are weighed against others' demands.

Individualistic ←————————————→ Communal

Mark on this spectrum where each of the following would fall: your community growing up, your family today, your workplace, and any other important settings in your life. How does this affect how you approach conflict?

. . . .
. . . .
. . . .
. . . .

Independence is encouraged in these cultures. Instead of relying on family and community for support, there are institutions that play that role, such as government structures, insurance companies, banks, and so forth. This means an individual can succeed more easily on their own, and there is less incentive to hold on to relationships when a conflict occurs. In many cases in individualistic societies, if the relationship does not work – in other words, if there is a stubborn conflict – one is free to end the relationship and find others to relate to.

In societies such as these, people may ask, "What's in it for me?" when deciding whether to resolve a conflict, escalate it, or make the effort to keep the relationship. Resolutions are often sought through formal processes, including courts and arbitrators, because people prefer structures, systems, and direct communication to navigating organic, relational modes of resolution.

On the other hand, in many non-Western societies (such as in Africa, Asia, and Latin America), the emphasis is on family and community. In these societies, the group's harmony is more important than the individual's desires. As a result, one is expected to participate in and maintain relations with the community. Being involved in networks of relationships leads to individual but, more importantly, communal benefits.

People depend on relationship networks and community to provide for each other's education, pay for medical bills, host weddings and funerals, support people in old age, and more. Therefore, everyone has a strong incentive to maintain harmonious relationships. Breaking off relationships has severe consequences in all areas of one's life.

In case of conflict, the individual is challenged, overtly or otherwise, to consider the benefits to others. Community interventions are common ways to resolve conflicts because harmony is crucial.

This is why an individual in more traditional societies will be expected to take further steps towards maintaining the relationship and seeking harmony.

There are exceptions, of course. For example, the Amish community in the United States is a collaborative group in the Western world that pursues harmony more than in non-Western communities; and there are individualists in non-Western societies, such as those in towns and cities in Africa, where relationships with tribal cultures are weakening.

Social norms such as individualism or communal harmony thus impact what kind of relationships we develop. They also influence our interests in maintaining or giving up on certain relationships whenever a conflict arises. Although these may be generalizations, understanding how you were raised helps you navigate relationships and conflicts.

What is your conflict style?

The conflict spiral suggests that there is more than one way to react to a situation – some that resolve conflict and some that escalate it. The appropriate response may differ based on the situation.

Studies show that we all react differently to conflict. We learn to react to conflict in predictable, almost habitual ways based on how we were brought up and our personalities. Our comfort level with conflict and what we consider an acceptable equilibrium also affects how we respond. These responses can be called our conflict styles or approaches. These become almost unconscious and our instinctive go-to approaches to any conflict situation, regardless of what might be most appropriate. Thankfully, these reactions can be trained so that we learn other ways to react.

A commonly used assessment can help you discover your habitual styles of dealing with conflict: the Thomas-Kilmann Inventory (TKI).

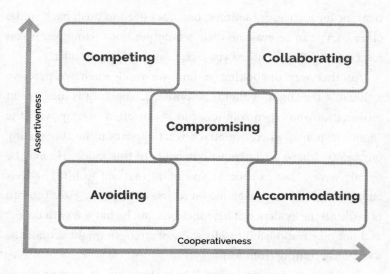

Named after two behavioural researchers, Dr Kenneth W. Thomas, and Dr Ralph H. Kilmann, this instrument helps people become conscious of their default reactions to conflicts. Adaptations of TKI tests may be available to take online for free.[1]

The TKI instrument assesses how much our typical reactions to conflict tend to be assertive/unassertive and cooperative/ uncooperative, and labels five different styles along those spectrums.

Competing, which is highly assertive and highly uncooperative, is when someone stands their ground and is determined to get their way. Competing means pushing back, arguing for our own solution, and defending ourselves. We may not want "to go down easily". We are convinced of our solution, rarely accept that we are wrong or need to change, and don't try to find common ground.

Competing is not always wrong, however. It can be a justified response when one needs to stand up for what one knows to be the

---

1 See, for example, the TKI Assessment instrument and other materials published Kilmann Diagnostics – https://kilmanndiagnostics.com

truth or for justice. Sometimes, one does need to push back so the other party can re-evaluate their wrong positions. However, if you react this way to all conflicts you face, relationships will suffer.

Another way of looking at how we react when we perceive a threat is the "fight or flight" response. Competing is focused on pushing for one's own solution, but it can often overlap with the "fight" response, where we attack what appears to be threatening our safety. I have a relative who defaults to this mode. He may be openly wrong, but as soon as you point that out to him, he feels emboldened to turn the blame on to you or someone else. You can provide all the evidence of his misdeeds, but he has a way to deflect and not take responsibility. His show of strength might actually be a response coming from fear.

Avoiding is unassertive and uncooperative. It sweeps issues under the carpet instead of confronting them. Think of the times when you had to drop a demand or give up on an issue even though you did not feel that your needs were met, or that the issue was properly addressed. Avoiding is a very common way to react when the stakes are low or when you want to avoid conflict you may consider unnecessary.

If fighting is like competing, taking flight is similar to avoiding, although it often involves a more physical or emotional withdrawal from the situation.

When you perceive a threat, flight can be used wisely as a preservation method to save yourself from abuse or being taken advantage of. When direct conflict with someone could put you in danger, removing yourself from the situation to protect yourself can be helpful. If necessary, you may approach the relationship later, from a safe distance.

Disengaging from the process for a time can allow you to collect yourself and think through the circumstances, but only if you come back with a reasonable approach to the conflict. If one or both parties permanently disengage, the result is a lose-lose situation because you don't get a chance to address the issues that led to the conflict in the first place. If either flight or avoiding is applied too often, this style leads to low-energy relationships and even broken trust. Few people want to be in a relationship where the other party withdraws or avoids dealing with issues.

Accommodating tends to be unassertive and low on cooperation. In this style, you allow the other person's views, interests, or positions to take precedence. It may be that you feel that your interests are not very important, or prefer to focus on unity rather than winning. Accommodating means that you have had to go along with another party's position or needs rather than fight for your own.

My default mode is accommodating, closely followed by avoiding. When I get into a conflict, especially with people close to me, I tend to look for ways towards a quick agreement. I'm not too fond of how conflict makes me feel emotionally. I am by nature – and now by training – a firm believer in living at peace with people, and therefore look to mend disagreements as soon as possible. Several of my close friends have challenged me to engage further before conceding to the other party's goals in a conflict. They argue that if I did not settle for peace so soon in every conflict situation, I would be able to hold on to my goals, including some which are noble.

In collaboration, which is highly assertive and highly cooperative, the parties seek a way forward together in order to resolve issues at the centre of their conflict. Collaborating involves reviewing the circumstances and working with the other party to resolve the issues, thereby transforming the relationship. The engagement can be intense because both parties are fully present. For collaboration, think of a time when you and the other party stayed engaged on

> **(?)**
>
> **Find an online TKI assessment link and take the test. Record your results below. Do you agree with these results? Why/why not?**
>
> ....
>
> ....
>
> ....
>
> ....

an issue until you could find a way forward, even if the solution was not what you initially anticipated or were pushing for.

This is often the preferred method to keep a relationship going. However, it should not be minimized as a soft or easier way to resolve conflict. In fact, it is often the most difficult, because parties need to face up to their contributions to the conflict in order to work out a way forward. They must also agree on how to move forward on the issues they were fighting about, which is no small task in some cases.

Compromise balances being assertive and cooperative. It involves an attempt to hear the other person out. While in accommodating or competing one person gets their way, this approach seeks common ground, but the result is not exactly what either party initially wanted. For compromise, think of taking this position when the value of the issues each side is pursuing is somewhat significant, but you both have flexibility and also want "peace". It can also be because you see how deeply the other side is entrenched in their position and see the value in their demand as more important than getting exactly what you want. You may also realize that continuing to push your point forward may mean the end of your relationship. People who overuse this style may be very focused on things being equal or fair and so try to force every disagreement into a precisely 50/50 resolution.

These default ways of reacting to conflict situations are learned and can form patterns in relationships with a particular individual. I see this a lot among married couples. Jim tends to react to his wife's displeasure by either walking away or shutting down – both of which are avoiding techniques. His wife, Carol, has realized that this is his way of doing things, so she tries to corner him in the evenings when he cannot walk away. She is being more assertive in order to make up for his lack of engagement. Unfortunately, this approach simply feeds the conflict. Jim does not want to be bothered, but Carol is equally determined to be heard. What results is a verbal argument.

No one style is necessarily better than another because each style has advantages, disadvantages, and uses in different circumstances, which we will explore in a future chapter. Our relationships are too complex to be treated only in one way. With study, you can find out what tends to be your default reaction and adjust so you are not tied to a particular way of doing things. Because each of these responses is learned, they can also be "unlearned". I have seen how this conflict styles assessment benefits people and equips them to transform their relationships.

A word of caution on assessments: no test can ultimately tell you this is who you are or how you always will be. We can change. Indeed, the goal of any test ought to be self-reflection and learning. It should help you determine growth areas and ways to develop beyond where you are today. For instance, since my TKI results are heavy on accommodating, I am training myself to be more assertive, especially on matters that are important to me.

A few words of caution are appropriate as you consider the above assessments. One, be aware that these assessments are enveloped within a broad cultural context, so be sure to factor your own cultural realities into the results. Maybe a woman tests primarily as compromising because, within her culture, women are taught to be submissive and to give in. Given her circumstances and cultural realities, a compromise might be the best option. Knowing your default reaction mode and the realities around you is helpful. The cultural envelope you are part of may remain the same, but you could learn how to operate best in that reality.

Two, never use the tests to analyse or assess another person. You are not qualified to make those judgements. It is best if each of us analyses ourselves and our results. So, please do not ask people to take the assessments and tell them what you think of their styles. You can come together with someone else (or a group) to analyse and discuss your results, but do that willingly, without judging the other. Remember, none of these styles is the best way to react to all conflict situations; that depends on many factors.

Our Communication

Communication is the only way to understand another person and for you to be understood. However, communication is also an important factor in starting, escalating, or de-escalating the conflict spiral.

Whether language or non-verbal communication, the goal is to send and receive meaningful messages that enable the sender and receiver to understand each other, to express ourselves, to share similar realities, and to make meaning.

Miscommunication can happen when the sending of the message is corrupted, such as poor word and expression choices, unclear information, or inaccuracies. To clear such a misunderstanding, review and clarify the message and what was understood or lost during the transmission.

Miscommunication can also happen when the receiving is corrupted, such as misinterpreting the communicator's message or intentions, often due to differing assumptions, perceptions, or perspectives. It can also be because of an intentional distortion of the information. If I dislike you for whatever reason (e.g., personality, background, or experience), I might choose to (mis)interpret whatever you say in a biased way. In this case, the message is not the problem, but rather what I choose to hear because of my own perceptions.

Communication also includes feedback on the messages received. As information is exchanged back and forth, miscommunications can quickly compound. Intentional miscommunication, quarrels, and abuse easily escalate conflicts. But unintentional miscommunication or outright misunderstanding can also lead to conflict. It is, therefore, crucial to learn how to communicate well to reduce unnecessary conflicts and de-escalate conflicts when they arise.

Yes, words can break bones

Conflicts involve words, whether mocking comments, shouting, swearing, demeaning names, or attacks on the character of the person. Indeed, in my experience as a mediator, I hear more about what people said – and how and why they said it – than what they actually did. That is because we remember hurtful words spoken to us and they affect us deeply, making relationships with the other party difficult. Words have the power to build but also to destroy.

How many times have you witnessed a careless word tear apart a relationship that you thought was strong? How do you feel when your boss scolds or yells at you? Or how did you feel when your contribution to a decision-making process was disregarded? It hurts when someone makes rude comments, berates you in public, spreads a rumour, or gossips about you. Unlike physical pain, which we alone feel, spreading gossip within the family or workplace spreads hurt among others. Many people's careers, families, and reputations (not to mention their egos) are destroyed by thoughtless words.

Indeed, "some people make cutting remarks, but the words of the wise bring healing" (Proverbs 12:18). That is why many verses in the Bible warn us to be careful in how we speak to others, such as: "Don't use foul or abusive language. Let everything you say be good and helpful, so that your words will be an encouragement to those who hear them" (Ephesians 4:29).

We are all in danger of saying careless words, especially when offended or disappointed by someone. But Jesus takes communication very seriously. He says, "And I tell you this, you must give an account on judgement day for every idle word you speak" (Matthew 12:36). While this may sound harsh, our words reflect the condition of our hearts. "A good person produces good things from the treasury of a good heart, and an evil person produces evil things from the treasury of an evil heart. What you say flows from what is in your heart" (Luke 6:45).

Jesus is saying that our speech reflects who we really are. This is both comforting and scary. It is comforting because it means we can change our conversations by grounding ourselves in "what is true, and honourable, and right, and pure, and lovely, and admirable" (Philippians 4:8). Jesus's argument is scary because my words in conflict expose who I really am. I can pretend, but won't the truth always come out?

You always/never . . .

Closely related to careless and cutting words are absolute words or ultimate condemnations. "You *always* forget to lock the door" or "you *never* appreciate *any* of my feelings". Perhaps the person forgot to do that a few times, but these statements exaggerate how often it happens. These comments declare the other party worse than they really are, suggesting they are incapable of better behaviour in any circumstance. "Always" and "never" express dismay with an individual's conduct and a determination that they are solely responsible for your hurt – something that cannot always be fully true.

Unfortunately, these exaggerations are common among people in close relations (e.g., family, or spousal relationships) where people feel freer to say what they think, especially if they have not learned to deal with one issue at a time and to keep a short account of each other's mistakes.

One can understand why such absolute terms are common in conflicts. When we are angry, our thought processes are not always under our full control and can be quite unreasonable. So we say things we would not otherwise say in calmer times, lose control, and end up attacking people or damaging property. Of course, there is no excuse for lacking self-control, but it helps to seek a better understanding of how we react when in a conflict. Then we can apply wisdom so that we do not say or do something we will regret later.

The silent treatment is conflict too

The silent treatment can also powerfully escalate a conflict. Threats, renunciations, and general non-cooperation falls in this area too. These manipulation tactics break down relationships.

The silent treatment is common among many spouses, but it also happens in neighbourhoods and in offices. An issue needs to be addressed, but someone decides to ignore the other person. This might be for a time (e.g., in a married relationship) or for ever (e.g., neighbours who choose not to ever talk again).

They may be offended by a comment or an action and, instead of engaging to clarify the comment or action, they shut down communication with the other person. The other party may not know what caused the silence. They may be perplexed and even try to engage the silent one without much success. I call this "the silent dance of wits". It is an attempt to control the other. The silent one often does not try to resolve or bring about some understanding. They are in control and will not let go until they have inflicted pain on the other party. Obviously, the silent one suffers too from the loss of relationship. Therefore, it can be just as injurious as the shouting and quarrelling described earlier.

Depending on the relationship, the issue may escalate to full disengagement and separation. The sooner the parties re-engage and have an honest conversation that resolves the issues, the better the chances of transforming that relationship. The lesson here, therefore, is to quickly learn what caused the offence, issue an apology, forgive, and make changes for future action.

The ABCs of how to get into conflict with almost anyone

There are many ways to get into conflict with other people. However, the following five behaviours are almost guaranteed to land you into a conflict with anyone, anytime.

How to get into conflict – fast		
Actions like . . . **(Description)**	**Words like . . .** **(Example)**	**Why this is** **unhelpful**
A = Argumentative		
• Bringing up past or unrelated issues to strengthen your case. • Trying to win for winning's sake, regardless of the facts. • Focusing on proving the other person wrong instead of trying to solve the problem.	• "You never do the right thing." • "You are making me insanely mad." • "What about the time you . . . ?" • "Why is it wrong for me to do this when you do it all the time?"	• Arguing makes people enemies. An issue today does not need to be compounded by linking it with others in the past if the goal is to manage the current conflict.
B = Blaming		
• Making excuses, not accepting your role in the conflict. • Characterizing the other as evil or guilty while exonerating yourself.	• "It is clearly your fault that we can't get along." • "You're the one who started this useless argument."	• Shifting blame does not address the problem. It also kills collaboration.

How to get into conflict – fast		
Actions like . . . (Description)	Words like . . . (Example)	Why this is unhelpful
B = Blaming (*continued*)		
• Demanding without discussion that others apologize because they are the ones who are wrong.	• "I had to act because you were dragging your feet." • "You know you are wrong. You'd better apologize if you want to be with me."	
C = Character Attacks		
• Name-calling, implying that the other person has poor morals or is unethical. • Putting the other down, insulting, stereotyping, or making them feel inferior. • Defamation or talking ill about the person to others.	• "I have never met a more incompetent person in my life." • "You are emotionally incapable of addressing issues." • "You are always absent-minded." • "How can you claim to be a Christian?" • "You men are always uncaring."	• Character attacks offer cheap excuses for the conflict – that the other party is inherently bad or evil – rather than looking at both sides and the root causes. It also causes a defensive response, derailing the discussion.
D = Disrespect		
• Showing open contempt, rudeness, or lack of courtesy towards others. • Interrupting or dismissing their views. • Intimidating someone by invading personal space, unwanted touch, or a raised voice.	• "Just how stupid does one have to be to not see this as an issue?" • "Would you shut up and stop your whining?"	• Disrespecting the other leads to distance. The person feels demeaned and unworthy, making them not engage honestly in the transformation process or making them angry and escalating emotions.
E = Evading		
• Walking away from issues or avoiding engagement. Silent treatment or shutting down a conversation by non-participation.	• "I don't want to talk about this. Leave me alone." • "Everything is okay." • "You're always making things up; this is no issue at all."	• Avoiding addressing issues does not make them go away; indeed, it piles them up for later.

After reviewing the ways that words can hurt, we can see why the biblical writer James compares the tongue to a fire (James 3:1-12). If mishandled, our communication can cause untold damage, just as fire can. In a conflict, we can use our words to wound deeply.

But James also says that the tongue can bless, meaning that it can be of great benefit. In a relationship, we can use our tongues to encourage others to grow, praise them, and offer our support. We can use words to heal: to mend the breach, solve problems, and share love and concern.

When we are able to understand the power of our words, we realize we need to train ourselves to wield them responsibly, to strengthen the bonds that hold us together. Yet James says that no human being can tame the tongue; we can only do so with God's help. Paul encourages us to "let your conversation be gracious and attractive so that you will have the right response for everyone." (Colossians 4:6).

Sin and Stopping the Spiral

If conflict often comes from differences – which can be neutral or good diversity – and if conflict can be a helpful way to learn and grow in relationships, how does it so easily tend toward destruction and violence?

In the New Testament, James asks a rhetorical question: "What is causing the quarrels and fights among you?" He answered with a question: "Don't they come from the evil desires at war within you?" (James 4:1). James acknowledges that our conflicts are rooted in our selfishness. Which of us can say we are not selfish? We all want to be comfortable and on our terms. Unfortunately, that may mean we are willing to fight for that comfort, sometimes even running over others.

In other words, our sinfulness causes our differences to escalate into harmful conflicts. Ever since Adam and Eve, we have underestimated our brokenness and selfishness. We quickly blame the other person and cast them as evil, while we excuse our sins as simple mistakes. Adam and Eve's rebellion against God broke the relationships between humans, God, and creation. A desire to control one another entered their relationship (Genesis 3:16).

Sin escalated the conflict between Adam and Eve's sons, Abel and his jealous older brother Cain. It began as a difference between the two brothers, who offered livestock versus crops to the Lord, and God accepted Abel's offering but not Cain's. Cain knew what to do to be accepted by God, because the Lord confronted him by saying, "Why are you so angry? . . . Why do you look so dejected? You will be accepted if you do what is right. But if you refuse to do what is right, then watch out! Sin is crouching at the door, eager to control you. But you must subdue it and be its master." (Genesis 4:6-7).

I have always considered this story sad as well as instructional. Sad because Cain was warned that his sin would destroy him. However, instead of correcting his course, he built up resentment and hatred against his brother. And I find it instructional because I often wonder how many sinful things I persist in even when I know they are damaging to me, my relationship with others, and God. Cain's conflict with Abel and God escalated because of Cain's sin of jealousy and his violent sin of murder. Eventually, sin escalated to the point that it destroyed the first human family and, in Noah's day, creation globally.

Cain's story illustrates how anger can lead to sin. Anger, like all other emotions, is an emotion created by God. It is a natural human reaction and may aid our relations in different ways. For example, we should rightfully be angry at injustice and sin wherever we see them. But we should be patient and hold back from using anger to lash out at others, manipulate relationships, or take revenge because "human anger does not produce the righteousness God desires" (James 1:20).

The Bible recognizes the tendency to react in anger as part of human weakness and warns us to work against the temptation to sin: "You must all be quick to listen, slow to speak, and slow to get angry" (James 1:19). "A gentle answer deflects anger, but harsh words make tempers flare" (Proverbs 15:1). Ephesians 4:26-27 warns that anger can lead to sin: "'Don't sin by letting anger control you.' Don't let the sun go down while you are still angry, for anger gives a foothold for the devil." This is not to say that we should never get angry, but rather that we should guard against reacting impulsively, especially in an emotional conflict. Human anger tends to escalate the conflict spiral.

It is unwise to jump into a conflict without paying attention to how we feel and what results our outbursts will likely bring about. Although an emotional outburst feels justified, it will be our worst enemy if our goal is to transform the relationship in a positive way. Some may argue that it is possible that the parties can release the tension within the relationship through yelling. I seriously doubt this is true. The last time you were angry and screamed at another person, can you honestly say you felt better afterward? I get more irritated, especially if the other person is yelling emotionally. No wonder the writer of the Proverbs warns, "Fools vent their anger, but the wise quietly hold it back" (Proverbs 29:11).

The good news is that even when Cain was angry, he had a choice about whether to sin or to control his anger. That we are sinful does not mean we are incapable of any good. It also does not mean we are doomed to sin or cannot see our sins. As Christians, through Jesus Christ, we have the power of the Holy Spirit to help us overcome sin and evil and to live at peace with others. We can choose how we react to conflicts and seek peaceful relations with others.

Often, the first step is controlling our anger. Try to develop the following skills:

1. When feeling angry, count to 10 before acting on your anger. Try doing this several times if needed.
2. Slow down and breathe deeply, slowly inhaling and exhaling. This should help calm your emotions.
3. Lower your voice and encourage yourself not to react to the other person if they are angry or shouting.
4. Where appropriate, distance yourself from the situation, but set a time to satisfactorily address the issues with the person when both of you are calm.
5. Look away or walk away from the environment – or the person causing the aggravation.

These techniques can pause the conflict spiral and even prevent emotional outbursts. When possible, take time to distance yourselves from the circumstances long enough to acquire healthier views about the other party and the incident. This objectivity may not be possible if we charge forward quickly or when emotions are high. If the parties come to the conflict with clear goals for what they want to get out of it, they are less likely to be yelling over each other. They may even engage each other more honestly and so move forward in a manner that is beneficial to everyone. The best result of applying this principle is transforming the conversation so everyone is listened to and heard.

Conclusion

As a conflict spirals out of control, it can become like a cyclone turning anything it encounters into a dangerous weapon. It is a furious fire that will burn and destroy. But the issue is not that we have differences of opinion or disagreements. It is how we react to those differences – whether we further entrench our positions or cooperate to address the issues with the other party, whether we use our conflict styles and communication to escalate or transform the conflict. We can harness the fire's energy for good uses such as cooking and purifying. Leaving conflicts unresolved risks scarring us or burning up our relationships. While not all conflicts can be resolved, we can determine to live in peace with others and transform our relationships. In the next chapter, we discuss how to move from fighting each other into fighting for valuable relationships.

Group Discussion

1. Think of a conflict you were part of that escalated. What were the original issues? What words and actions caused the conflict to grow?
2. Map specific words and actions onto the conflict spiral to show what fuelled the fire at each step. What opportunities could have been taken to de-escalate at each step?

Study the ABCs table on how to get into conflict with almost anyone. What are some of your areas of weakness? How could you do the opposite to get out of conflict? Write these positive actions and words in the table below. For instance, instead of blaming, what words could you say to take responsibility?

How to get out of conflict – fast	
Actions like . . . (Description)	Words like . . . (Example)
A = ~~Argumentative~~ Focusing on solving the current issue	
B = ~~Blaming~~ Taking Responsibility	
C = ~~Character Attacks~~ Focusing on actions	
D = ~~Disrespect~~ Respect	
E = ~~Evading~~ Actively engaging	

3

Fight for Relationships

sabela and Moria had moved to the United States with their two children. Isabela qualified and started to work as a nurse while Moria continued his graduate studies. They dealt with the stress of Moria's studies and all the required tuition for eight years. Isabela also worked night and weekend shifts, making the situation at home very stressful. The family hardly had time together. Upon graduating with a PhD in leadership, Moria tried to find work, but the country's economy was so bad that he could not find any substantive employment. Although he considered it beneath his training, he started to drive for Uber to help make ends meet. But still this was not enough money for his family. Two of his kids were now in college and needed significant financial support.

The stress Moria was experiencing seemed to seep into his relationship with Isabela as well. She wanted him to get a better job that would allow her to reduce her hours as a nurse. But there were no jobs available. Now that he was no longer a student, his visa was also due to expire, and he would not be able to work legally in the country. After a while, he became discouraged.

"I am going back home," Moria announced to Isabela.

"What do you mean you are going home?" she asked.

"You and the kids can stay here, in the US. I will go back home and find work there. My friends tell me it is possible to be hired at one of the local universities. I will see how it works. I can come to visit sometimes. You can also bring the kids to visit me."

"So, your mind is made up?"

"Yes, and I want to leave as soon as possible."

"Okay," Isabela said, resigned to Moria's decision.

Moria left the next month for Malawi, their home country. He knew returning to the US would be difficult without a job and legal status.

Once back in Malawi, he taught at a private university in the capital. The salary could have been better, but he had a regular income and could retain his dignity.

Back in the US, Isabela found work with a travelling nursing company that would also apply for her immigration papers, which meant that her husband could return to the country whenever possible. But that would take several years, and they would be apart all that time.

After six lonely years of separation, the visa papers finally came through. Isabela was excited that they would be reunited. She then travelled with the kids, who had graduated from college by this time, to visit Moria. However, by this time, Moria had settled down in their home country, been promoted several times, and was now the Deputy Chancellor at the university. This felt like the wrong timing to leave for the States. Isabela did not, however, want to move back home. Her life and the kids' lives were in the US.

Their conversations during the visit were tense. After two weeks without an agreement, Isabela and the kids returned to the US. Moria was torn. He wanted to keep his family together but could not just pick up and leave. Isabela had given him a firm ultimatum that he needed to return to the US to stay married.

No More Disposable Relationships

Conflicts can be so destabilizing that they make us question the value or necessity of the relationship. The issue can demand so much of our focus that we must find out why we should stay in the relationship long enough to weather the conflict.

In mediation, I often ask the parties involved to describe how much they want to fight for their relationship and why. I am always surprised how many cannot answer that question with a definite "Yes, I am willing to fight for this relationship despite what it may take." In these circumstances, the individual often focused more on how to walk away from the relationship than what would build it back up.

A long-term commitment to relationships couldn't be more needed than right now. Our societies seem to be disposing of relationships more easily than ever before. The goal of relationships is to make "me happy"; if that cannot happen, then I need to move on. Also, people tend to blame others, calling them toxic or incompatible, often as an excuse to disengage. Sometimes, it is they who are unwilling to do the hard work of finding a way forward together or are not self-critical enough. Even long-term relationships like marriage and business partnerships are unfortunately being reduced to "What can I get out of this relationship?"

If a relationship is about what you are getting out of it, it's easy to say, "If it does not work for me, there is no reason to stay." Regrettably, many relationships – from marriages to family relationships to friendships – suffer because people lack a commitment to the core beliefs of why they are involved with one another. When we ask ourselves, "How does it make me happy or fulfilled?" rather than saying, "I will build this for the long term, with all its joys and pains," we evaluate our relationships according to unrealistic standards, causing countless unnecessary breaks of essential relationships.

To work through a conflict, you need to hold on to hope that that relationship is worth fighting for. Articulate why the relationship is essential. Remind yourself why you value relationships. Instead of focusing on what you get out of it, if your goal is to serve the other and grow together, you will desire to repair the hurt and seek a way forward. A commitment to the relationship that stems from a deep desire to make it survive or thrive will always demand more profound effort and further action to rescue it from current conflicts.

Working through the difficulties associated with issues you might be dealing with will require persistence. Most of us work at things we value with passion and commitment that helps us grow. This chapter reminds us of why we need to value relationships and suggests some practical ways to do that. When we commit to our relationship, both parties benefit, we grow into more selfless and caring people, and we build lasting bonds in families and societies.

This does not mean that the commitment is easy. It can be especially difficult when we do not get the benefit from the relationship that we initially imagined. A long-term view, which often diverges from personal gain and the acceptable societal view, is the only guarantee that we can weather the tough times that conflict brings to our relationships.

Why Commit to Relationships?

Relationships are rewarding

But why commit to our relationships? Relationships are worth holding on to because they are rewarding in the long term. However, I don't mean to imply that we get into relationships only to harvest one-sided or self-serving benefits. We all know people who get close to us because they want something or some networking connection we have, and when we don't or are unable to provide what they need, they disappear. Perhaps a charming guy wants to be friends with a woman, but he takes off as soon as she refuses to sleep with him.

We do not need to take a selfish view of relationships to still affirm that we all benefit from relationships: enjoyment, sharing mutual interests, and companionship. We are created to be in communion with others. Our lives cross and connect with others. We serve and are served by others. When we reduce relationships to expectations of benefits, we ignore that our relationships are already valuable to us in many ways – and will continue to be. You have probably heard about the *ubuntu* concept, popularized by the late Archbishop Emeritus Desmond Tutu of South Africa – the idea that "I am because we are." In other words, my well-being is dependent on other people's humanity. I cannot be all-sufficient in and of myself. Among the Meru people of eastern Kenya, this concept is expressed by a saying that shares the same linguistic root, "*antu ibo into*," literally meaning, "people are the wealth." This means you are not wealthy unless you are in a relationship with others. Similar sayings in other parts of Africa recognize the primary importance of relationships in their various forms. Humanity is better off primarily due to our ability to form and nurture relationships with others, both short-term and long-term.

I grew up on a farm, growing tea and other crops and raising domestic animals. Even today, I love gardening, watching the plants

> (?)
>
> **What sayings does your community have that extol the need for better relationships, similar to "*antu ibo into*"?**
>
> ....
>
> ....
>
> ....
>
> ....

grow, and enjoying the vegetables and fruits. As a farmer, you need knowledge that will deliver the best harvest. Each plant has its favoured growing season, soil type, spacing, fertilizers, pesticides, pruning, and care. How and when you harvest tomatoes and potatoes are different. For permanent crops, like tea, the farmer must consider where to put them and nurture them so that they will thrive in the long term.

Given all this work and care, every farmer I know will tell you that farming is not for the fainthearted. It takes time, effort, knowledge, and much patience. Strangely, you can do very little to make plants grow. You can prepare the soil, sow the seed, water, fertilize, and even weed. But plants have their season and time of growth programmed within and cannot be rushed. You can kill the plant by overwatering, using too much fertilizer, or neglecting it; but you cannot speed up its growth process. The harvest comes when it needs to come, and no sooner.

I like to think of relationships in much the same way. They need care, effort, and other investments – in time, encouragement, and commitment. I need to provide the right environment for them to flourish, protect them against anything that would harm them, and celebrate ongoing harvests where possible. Effort in dealing with hurt, repentance, and forgiveness is like pruning. Guarding against pests and destructive elements, I equate to protecting my relationships from attitudes and perceptions that can damage what we try to build. By patiently tending to the relationships in the long term, I expect to – and indeed do – enjoy the fruits of many of them. However, I also need to be realistic that those fruits are not guaranteed, require the hard work of tending to the relationship, and cannot be forced.

Consider a parent-child relationship. Young children are notorious for doing or saying the wrong things. It takes a lot of patience, guidance, and discipline to get them to where they know and do what is right. I could not help noticing how often my friends had to say "no" or "don't" to their two-year-olds in the hour I was visiting them. Their daughter was prone to getting into trouble. Her attention seemed to lead her everywhere in her discoveries, including potentially harmful things like touching a hot stove. Her parents might have felt discouraged when they realized their most common word to her was "no".

The day-to-day efforts required to mould and protect your children can be exhausting, but they shouldn't overshadow the overall goal. Eventually, when my friends' daughter is grown like my adult sons, they will know the sheer joy of sharing a great relationship with their adult children, which is worth all the effort of the earlier years. A long-term view motivates parents to overcome a frustrating child-rearing process.

Good relationships, like fruitful gardens or mature children, take time to build and nurture. Taking a long view of the relationship means that parties are willing to overlook current circumstances (including mistakes or hurts) and consider the benefits of their bond in the long term. What we are going through today is all part of an overarching journey together. The day-to-day events only work when considering the complete view of life together.

Of course, as humans, we are limited in how much we can see beyond the current situation, so we are tempted to use short-term cost-benefit analyses to determine what we should do or what kind of choices to make. In a conflict, I encourage you to consider the long-term implications of relationship-related decisions. Your choices could have significant ramifications for your ongoing relationship with someone else.

God is committed to relationship

We have significant biblical encouragement on how and why we should work for our relationships, putting as much effort as possible into saving and growing them. First, God created humans out of love (Genesis 1:26). When humans sinned, causing a conflict, God's solution was to love us, his enemies. He provided for their immediate needs, covering their shame of nakedness by clothing Adam and Eve. He also gave them a way out of their decision to defy God and threaten the relationship. But God promised to strike down Satan through Jesus and restore the broken relationship (Genesis 3:15).

God did everything he could to restore the relationship. In Christ, God died to atone for the sins of Adam and Eve's descendants and their brokenness (John 3:16). He is the promised redemption at the break of the relationship, "the Son of Man came not to be served but to serve others and to give his life as a ransom for many" (Matthew 20:28). "He himself is the sacrifice that atones for our sins – and not only our sins but the sins of all the whole world" (1 John 2:2). We know that Jesus (God) did this willingly and out of love in order to restore humanity to a better relationship; he did it not out of compulsion (John 10:18). "Because of the joy awaiting him, he endured the cross, disregarding its shame. Now he is seated in the place of honour beside God's throne" (Hebrews 12:2). For the sake of sinful humanity, Jesus took the cost of the human-God conflict on himself. Indeed, as Isaiah had prophesied, "he was pierced for our rebellion, crushed for our sins. He was beaten so we could be whole. He was whipped so we could be healed" (Isaiah 53:5). He reconciled the relationship.

Finally, let us consider God's abiding patience with humanity and the choice to focus on a long-term relationship with us. It would have been right and just for God to destroy Adam and Eve when they sinned and then to recreate humanity. They were his creation, and he could do as he wanted with them. Similarly, God could choose to destroy us when we sin or reject him. He came close to doing just that at the time of Noah through the flood. Reading through the prophets, you get the sense that God, even though he hates sin, is loving and eager to restore his people if only they will repent and return to a relationship with him. As Peter indicates, God is gracious, not wanting us to perish (2 Peter 3:9). He offers us second (and many other) chances to repent and return to love and relationship. God is patient with us, and his perspective is aimed at eternity – a truly long-term goal.

God is patient and forgiving of our weaknesses, mistakes, and disappointments. He keeps returning to re-establish those relationships with us, hoping we will stay and live with him for eternity. This is a beautiful example of how we should envision our relationships with other people.

I want to be careful not to say that everyone should imitate God's level of self-sacrifice in every one of our relationships with others because that is impossible. In another chapter, we will talk about caveats to applying this situation, such as in abusive contexts. But God's own self-sacrifice does challenge us to be more willing to sacrifice beyond what would be our natural selfish motivation. Even when someone else hurts us deeply, Christians are called to love our enemies and trust that God will ultimately judge us all justly. Our sacrifice is possible because we know God has already willingly sacrificed the same for us.

How Do We Commit to Relationships?

Assume it depends on you

Paul encourages us to emulate God's character in this way. For me, Romans 12:18-21 is the guiding scripture of this whole book:

Do all that you can to live in peace with everyone.

Dear friends, never take revenge. Leave that to the righteous anger of God. For the Scriptures say,

"I will take revenge;
I will pay them back,"
says the LORD.

Instead,

"If your enemies are hungry, feed them.
If they are thirsty, give them something to drink.

In doing this, you will heap
burning coals of shame on their heads."

Don't let evil conquer you, but conquer evil by doing good.

"Do all that you can to live in peace with everyone." Assume that the relationship depends entirely on you. Your attitudes, comments, actions, and way of doing things all impact the future of any relationship you are part of. Take the perspective that says, "I want this to work. I want to fight for this relationship." This means that instead of walking away so quickly when there is a disappointment, seek ways to restore the relationship, keep it going, and transform it.

The most significant mental shift in "do all that you can to live in peace" might be realizing that we can change ourselves, not others. Consider how Adam and Eve passed the blame for sinning and breaking their relationship with God and each other. Often people will accuse and demand the other to change. Psychologists have studied this phenomenon for many years and concluded that this demand leads to you feeling unduly justified to continue the fight but does not address the issues that led to the break in the first place.

However, if you shift the focus to yourself and decide to take responsibility for your part in the conflict, there is often the hope that the parties may find a better way forward. It takes humility and courage to own up to your side of the mistake, but there is power in reversing that spiral and accepting responsibility. Take the lead in growing, protecting, and restoring your relationships. There is hope when we come into the conflict conversation aiming to understand and heal the relationship, and we assume that we are the ones responsible for making that happen.

Affirm the relationship

How do we avoid doubting or blaming others when things go wrong, especially in conflict?

One way to do this is to start by affirming the relationship's importance and committing to each other's and the relationship's growth. The commitment recognizes the possibility (maybe even the certainty) of disagreements. But it pledges to treat these as opportunities for growth for self and the relationship. This is part of choosing the "we" instead of the "I." Our relationship becomes about more than our shared interests and desires. That does not mean we forsake our individuality, personal goals, or interests. Of course, there are situations where one of us needs to be listened to, and our interests or position takes priority. But even in those cases, we do that in a way that affirms and supports the relationship's well-being. Focusing on shared goodwill between the parties helps provide a positive way forward. It becomes "you and me together against the problem."

> **(?)** Choose one relationship you care about. What drew
> you together? What is valuable about the relationship
> that you want to protect regardless of conflicts?
>
> ....
> ....
> ....
> ....

To carry out this principle, try focusing on what drew you together. Determine the critical aspects of the relationship you want to protect beyond the conflict you're experiencing now. This helps you avoid being sucked into attitudes that can destroy what you have been building. When both parties adopt the mindset, "I will do my best to labour for this relationship whatever the cost", you can almost always save the relationship.

For example, in our earlier case study, Moria and Isabela need to define the importance of the family and why they need to be together. Moria is weighing whether to leave his job, with the sense of security and meaning it provides, to rejoin his wife across the globe so that they can continue building their family together. Creating a family is what brought them together in the first place. Choosing to give up his career to have an opportunity to rebuild his marriage is no small sacrifice.

I understand that making these choices may not always be possible. For example, I know many people whose jobs or immigration status have meant being separated from their families for a long time, much of it against their will. They would do anything possible to change this but cannot. However, where one has an alternative, protecting and sustaining the relationship's primary goal is truly beneficial.

Grow your conflict competence

Sometimes our commitment to relationships suffers because we are so committed to our point of view on an issue. We assume that one of us must be right and the other must be wrong. We don't know any other way of handling conflict and cannot risk being wrong, so we sacrifice our relationships and end up with poor outcomes.

To avoid this, we can develop our conflict competence. This is our ability to understand and approach conflicts masterfully, with curiosity and a focus on constructive transformation. This is the commitment to embrace the sweet middle versus swinging to the extremes of conflict. We are willing to learn and change instead of sticking to only what we currently know. We learn about the basic dynamics of conflicts, the best processes of engagement, and appropriate steps toward transformation. Managing expectations and emotions, understanding self, and learning better listening and response skills –all concepts I explore in this book – are the basics we need to move towards conflict competence.

Conflict competency is the skills, knowledge, and attitudes to identify, understand, and manage conflicts effectively. This can include:

- Active listening and effective communication skills to understand the perspectives and needs of all parties involved in a conflict;
- Empathy and understanding of different cultures, values, and backgrounds to help bridge differences and build mutual understanding;
- Creative problem-solving and negotiation skills to develop mutually acceptable solutions to conflicts;
- The ability to remain calm and objective, even in difficult or high-pressure situations;
- The ability to reflect on one's biases and assumptions to avoid perpetuating conflicts; and

- Knowledge and understanding of the dynamics of power
  and privilege to address inequality and social justice issues.

Conflict competency is important for organizations and individuals if they wish to achieve goals and objectives, create positive and healthy work environments, and improve relationships. This knowledge can be built into attitudes, beliefs, and processes appropriate for transforming conflict. Of course, this comes with extensive practice, with different levels of success and failure. But that is true of anything we hope to learn and perfect. It is the same with using a fire, especially for constructive purposes like baking, cooking, or heating. Through experience, you learn when to use a stronger flame and when to reduce it so it can just simmer the food. Conflict competence helps us not to fear conflict but to learn how to engage it thoughtfully and confidently. This book teaches you to appreciate conflict, transform it, and build your relationships. I will develop these ideas for the rest of the book.

Building before You're in Flight

You may have heard the expression, "building while the plane is flying," which means coming up with solutions to problems only once you are in the middle of an endeavour. Of course, you can't build a plane while flying. In an emergency, you must patch up things as you go until you can land the plane safely. Sometimes, this is also the case in some of our relationships, where we are caught unawares when a conflict arises, so we must improvise a reaction. But it should not be our default mode to only ever fix things on the fly.

When we begin a relationship, we seldom consider conflict with that person. But relationships, especially if they span some time and are committed, will inevitably experience some form of conflict. When you are in the midst of an emotional conflict, you will wish you had taken steps to prepare beforehand.

Of course, there is no way to anticipate all the issues that will arise in all your relationships. But you can take a few critical preventative steps to prepare you better for when you (inevitably) find yourselves in conflict.

Build up a deposit of goodwill

Goodwill needs to be built throughout a relationship, not just drawn out of thin air when required. Just as we deposit money into or withdraw it from our bank accounts, we can also deposit trust into our relationships, providing credit for future needs. Suppose there are too many withdrawals and too few deposits. When more significant issues arise, we find it challenging to work through those issues because we have exhausted the support and trust we could otherwise have used. Deposits and withdrawals can be built in good times and times of conflict.

For another example, I used to run cross country when I was in high school. I can't say I was very good at it, but I tried. In training, one of the key lessons for running a long race was to consider how long you would be running, then adjust your speed and pace accordingly. Otherwise, you might take off too fast and tire before you can complete the race. Or, you might run too slowly to ever win.

This is excellent advice for relationships. Long-term relationships take a consistent pace of commitment, constant sacrifice, and building and protecting trust. They may demand a longer view of developing necessary agreements and ways of acting with and around each other. There is no benefit to an aggressive "sprint" of fighting in order to gain resolution on an issue – you will not win in the end. One can practise kindness and achieve the same goals.

Agree on an engagement framework

If you can craft a framework before you take off and fly, you will increase the likelihood of a better outcome if (when!) problems arise. The plan does not have to be exhaustive but to give you guidelines to work out the issues when they arise. Agreeing on a conflict engagement framework is one of the best prevention tools to safeguard a relationship. It is also a wise way to plan for the relationship's growth because you are determining the direction you want to go and what to avoid by developing a plan.

The more crucial the relationship, the more you want to be prepared for eventualities. High-stakes relationships – like marriage, business partnerships, and property ownership – can and do go wrong. When they do, there are enormous consequences. Many people are shocked by how difficult it is to determine a conflict engagement framework while in the middle of a conflict when everything is suddenly much more personal. Therefore, it is prudent to prepare and agree on a strategy for dealing with issues that will arise. In some of these (e.g., business partnerships), the partners hire lawyers to help craft mediation or arbitration frameworks for when things do not work as intended.

Although my wife and I had courted for three years, early in our marriage, we ran into issues about money, decisions on how to raise kids, and where to live, for instance. These were all things we had been advised about in our premarital counselling, but there was no way to anticipate the specifics of each of their complexities. We needed more than the simple belief that things would work out and that we could always agree on all issues.

After hitting these bumps a few times, my wife and I realized we needed general agreements on approaching issues when they arose. So we crafted a framework for addressing problems when we disagreed on the way forward. We wrote only the outlines of our framework, which meant we often negotiated as we encountered conflict situations. Over the years, as our lives changed, we modified these agreements to include other needs.

Below I share some outlines of part of our initial framework. You can use part or all of this as a starting point to develop your own. Also, the principles outlined in this book are an expanded part of this framework. The principles affirm the need to address, not avoid, conflict.

> We commit to always deal with each other honestly, to develop our love and commitment to each other by investing in our relationship, to always trust each other, and to keep the goal of growing our relationship in mind. When in disagreement, we will refrain from blaming the other, quarrelling, and seeing the other as the enemy. Instead, we will try to listen to that person's side of the story. We will work diligently towards an agreement on the issue at hand and not let history crowd our judgement. This might require giving up on our views and positions for the sake of the relationship. If we cannot agree on a way forward, we will hold off from a decision unless one must be made. We will always remember that we are friends and trust each other. Developing this goodwill between us is the most important gift we can give each other.

As you can see, these are broad goals, committing to the relationship and laying down how to grow even through times of conflict. For the most part, this framework has worked as intended (when we are calm enough to remember it!), mainly because it helps us engage each other around issues. They remind us why we are engaged with the other person, what it will take to keep the relationship going, and what steps to take toward resolving conflicts.

It is important to note that business relations differ significantly from interpersonal relationships, so they need different agreements.

There are plenty of resources to help with maintaining good business relationships. Additionally, these relations are subject to local, national, and even international contract laws. Numerous guidelines exist for forming partnerships and relationships specific to your business and context. So, review whatever laws apply to you in your context and let them guide you in your business relationships.

Ultimately, I recommend having a defined conflict engagement framework in place, one you sign on as binding and can fall back on when needed. For higher levels of investment, it would be best if this were legally binding. This helps cover all the bases should you end up with disagreements. Since much of this is relatively dependent on individual situations, I do not provide an example here; however, here are some questions that can guide you as you commit to a business relationship, and primarily how you address a conflict.

- What arrangements do we have for addressing any issues that come up?
- Who will be our contact person as a step forward if we cannot agree between ourselves?
- Are courts and other legal mechanisms open for us, or should we turn to them only after we have exhausted our interpersonal processes – including using a mediator?

Several years ago, I saw this principle masterfully applied by two business friends involved in the secondhand-clothes business. One partner was to provide the investment cash, and the other would work full-time in the business. They had been friends from an early age, having grown up together. But when forming the company, they recognized the possibility of conflict, which could end their friendship. This was because money was involved, and one partner would need to trust the other, who would handle most of it.

They sought a trusted mutual friend to help them protect their friendship as well as the business partnership. Together, they established a set of agreements about the business and their friendship and a procedure to follow if they had disagreements about their business. Their friend committed to being a listening ear whenever needed. Questions about the business have arisen occasionally, but the two partners have resolved these based on the goodwill of their friendship and their pre-drafted procedure for resolutions. It is no wonder that both their friendship and their partnership have survived.

All relationships need maintenance and repair. If you are close enough to anyone, you will rub up against each other and sometimes rub each other the wrong way. But conflict does not need to destroy and can even transform relationships when we aim to protect or renew the relationship. The Bible encourages us to take responsibility to do all we can to live in peace, just as God did (and does) with us. We can do this by affirming the importance of the relationship, focusing on what brought us together, preparing for conflict, and building on our trust.

Conclusion

Isabela came from a broken home and feared the struggle of living alone in a foreign country. When she confided in a friend that she was contemplating divorce, her friend introduced her to a lawyer to process the divorce. However, before filing the papers, Isabela decided to call Moria and give him one last chance. He was welcome to return in the next three months, or she would proceed with the divorce.

When he received Isabela's ultimatum, Moria was torn. He could stay and continue to rise in his career and lose his family – or vice versa. He went to see his pastor for advice. The pastor was candid; he encouraged him to resign and follow his wife. This, however, was not the advice Moria wanted. He thought the pastor would tell him to force Isabela to return home.

He confided in the friend who had been his best man when he married Isabela. His friend reminded him how he had watched their courtship. "Remember all the things you used to tell me you loved about Isabela? The two of you have been through a lot together. No one else knows you as she does." Moria realized that, although he tried to push through and not think about it too often, he missed his wife and children. The joy and intimacy they had once shared now seemed like a distant memory, but maybe there was still hope for them. While he knew there were no guarantees that he would be able to save their future, he had to do something about where they were at right now.

After struggling with the decision for another nine months, Moria resigned, packed his bags, and joined his wife in the US. He was returning to unemployment, trying to heal his relationship with his wife and children, and rebuilding what was lost after being apart for seven years. But, as he confided in his friend before he left for the US, "My family is more important than all the money in the world. I will do whatever it takes to keep us together."

Instead of asking, "What can I get out of this?" when deciding how much to commit to the relationship, imagine what would happen if we asked, "What can I give to preserve this relationship? How can I resolve this conflict?" That does not mean, even when we value our relationships, that the efforts to transform conflict will be easy. It all takes a lot of effort. Developing skills around conflict and having tools like a pre-agreement framework to follow when conflict arises will help you to navigate the process better if the goal is to save and grow the relationship.

The next chapter explores practical ways to apply this commitment to saving and growing our relationships during conflict. We can and should approach conflict with the goal to move us forward positively.

Think of a close relationship you have, whether with your spouse, roommate, family member, or colleague. Take time to develop a framework for you to use when needed. Be sure to tailor it to your needs and make it an adaptable living document.

....

....

....

....

....

....

....

....

....

....

....

....

Group Discussion

1. What is the prevailing messaging in your community, past and current, about the importance of relationships? Use your cultural context as the point of discussion.

2. What is the biblical view of relationships? How does this messaging compare to your community or context today? Why are committed relationships essential today?

Choose a Path Forward

Atwoli lived most of his life in the city. He had moved there over 25 years previously when he got a job at a bakery. He learned quickly and eventually became the master baker.

Before moving to the city, Atwoli had had two children with Akinyi, a woman from the neighbouring village. Per the customs of their tribe, Akinyi had moved in to live on Atwoli's family property. Atwoli had built her a small house next to his parents. After moving to the city alone, he would visit the village around Christmas every year and stay with Akinyi for about a week. Otherwise, he lived in the city most of the time. As years passed, Akinyi and Atwoli had more children. As was customary, Atwoli would come home for the naming ceremony after the birth but, given his role at the bakery, he would not stay in the village for any extended time. Akinyi was lucky because she had her mother-in-law and several other relatives to help with the children. Atwoli also sent enough money home monthly to support the family.

In the city, Atwoli met Mumbi, a lovely lady who worked as an attendant in the local bar, which he frequented some evenings. Mumbi bore Atwoli a son and, for the next 20 years, they lived together and had other children. Mumbi knew that Atwoli had a wife in the village. She did not mind his once-a-year trips to the village but insisted that she wanted their relationship to be considered legitimate under the law. So they went to the city courthouse and got certified as married.

But then Atwoli died suddenly. He went to work one morning and collapsed in the bakery kitchen. The other workers tried to revive him but to no avail. The bakery owner called to let Mumbi know Atwoli was dead. Mumbi decided to have him buried in the city cemetery. When word reached Akinyi and the family in the rural home that Atwoli had died, they immediately sent Atwoli's eldest brother and Atwoli's son to the city to find out about the funeral process. Custom demanded that every male be buried in the village where he was born – next to his ancestors.

When they met with Mumbi, she told them that she was the legal wife and had the right to bury her husband wherever she wanted. She was not going to let them interfere with her plans. She ordered the mortuary not to let anyone see or take Atwoli's body. She also demanded half the piece of land where the family lived since that had belonged to Atwoli.

Atwoli's son and brother were confounded. They had come intending to bring the body back to the village. However, Mumbi was now standing in the way of that plan. They consulted with tribespeople in the city. They offered to help the family sue Mumbi for the right to have the body released to them so that they could give Atwoli a proper traditional burial in the village alongside his ancestors.

Start with a Goal in Mind

The stakes were high in the conflict between Mumbi's and Akinyi's families. They needed to think carefully about their goals in order to determine how to respond. What was most valuable to them? What outcomes were possible? What flexibility and constraints did each of them have?

In this chapter and the next, we will discuss achievable goals regarding conflict outcomes and how to determine where you want to go. Imagine, as is common with teenagers, you and your friends decided to walk to the next town/village just for fun. You weren't precisely sure why you were going along. What if your expectations were not met once you arrived? You may even have been accosted by kids from the other village. On the way back, a few people voiced their displeasure with the trip, but no one had been brave enough to say anything when the group initially set out. It might have saved you a lot of time and maybe even pain if you had all agreed on why you were making the trip in the first place.

In much the same way, it is better to approach a conflict situation with a goal or goals. Both research and practice affirm that we do better in our relationships, especially when navigating conflict if we have clear goals for the connection. Clarifying expectations and setting new goals are often part of resolving a conflict. To do this well requires honesty between the parties about why they are engaged with each other and what they want from the relationship.

Most of us are caught off guard when a relationship starts to deteriorate, especially in an emotional conflict, because we do not have specific goals for those relationships. Our initial reaction to conflict is often surprise or shock. As a result, we may leap into attack-or-react mode, acting counterproductively to what we want. We seldom take the time to evaluate where we want the relationship to go.

If we take the time to prepare and understand the issues, we can figure out how we should proceed. What do we want out of the engagement with the other person? Asking ourselves a few questions can help us determine possible resolutions, how much effort to invest in resolving the conflict, and what steps to take next. I encourage people to explore these questions mentally or in writing when in a conflict.

As you work through each question, you will learn steps to transform the relationship in order to set out on an intentional path in the right direction.

How Open Are They to Cooperation?

The first set of questions is:

- How open is the other party to cooperation?
  - What is the level of commitment of the other party?
  - What results can I realistically expect from the conflict?

Sometimes, you approach the other party with an offer to collaborate, and they initially refuse. I remember working in an office where one of our colleagues was considered a "difficult person". He was argumentative, unafraid to fight, and easily upset about almost everything. Unfortunately, although he was a good worker, he was among the first to be laid off when staff reduction came around. I am confident that part of the consideration to fire him was because so many people complained about not getting along with him.

Although it is often done, we must be careful about labelling people as "difficult". Of course, people can be stubborn and display problematic behaviours – whether because of their personality or their sinful attitude – but that is not really who they are. When we apply any label to someone we are in conflict with, they will inevitably feel attacked and judged. As a result, they will be less willing to engage with you to find a solution to your conflict. In fact, by labelling them, you might make them more challenging!

Suppose you meet someone who seems to have a lot in common with you. But as you try to develop a relationship, they continually point out the faults they see in you. Or, even when the facts demonstrate that they are wrong, they are unwilling to take a second look and own up to their mistakes. This behaviour can stall conflict transformation. If the other person will not engage with you to resolve whatever issues you have and build the relationship further, it becomes hard to collaborate.

But, as discussed in the last chapter, the Bible tells us to do everything in our power to try to transform this relationship. In other words, do not just walk away. Stay put and engage. Don't assume that because the person is exhibiting difficult behaviour, that is a licence for you to take off and not continue trying. Maybe they are not ready to engage at this point but will do so in the future. Sometimes, it is good to take a break and come back to see whether it is possible to engage further.

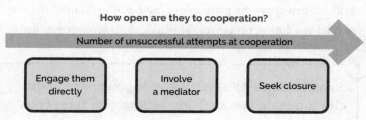

How open are they to cooperation?

Number of unsuccessful attempts at cooperation

Engage them directly

Involve a mediator

Seek closure

Since this question is about the other person's willingness to engage, you can seldom answer it for them. Instead, you must figure it out by engaging with the other person. You can start by inviting the other person to collaborate and then, if they are unwilling to cooperate, gradually draw in more help. Eventually, you may need to withdraw from them, but only after going through an intentional process to seek an agreed resolution. When we fail to pursue these steps and cut the relationship off too quickly, we miss out on the richness of relationships, jumping around between various short-term relationships, and our society becomes more fragmented. We also miss out on the growth we could have experienced through conflict and learning more about ourselves.

Engage them directly

To determine how open the other person is to collaborating and resolving your conflict, there is a helpful set of steps you can take to choose the appropriate resolution. In Matthew 18, Jesus teaches a process for engaging with someone who has sinned against you. Jesus specifically talks about a situation in which a fellow believer has wronged another. Some conflicts don't involve sin but merely someone's approach to a dispute or a different opinion. In other conflicts, the parties may not have a shared worldview about what is morally wrong. In other disputes, *both* parties may have sinned against each other.

Still, we can apply the principle of gradually escalating the scope to conflict resolution processes. This model involves engaging with

Read Matthew 18:15-17. What do you notice about the suggested process for dealing with someone who has wronged you?

someone directly, then involving a mediator, and then involving the community where necessary. It provides a way forward that ensures that the measures increase gradually and only to the level of non-cooperation displayed by the other party.

Jesus explains that if someone is at fault or causes you harm, you should go to them and point out the sins they have committed against you. See if you can convince them to work things out. This would be just between the two of you; if the person listens, the issue is resolved.

Here is how I have used this in a conflict resolution process. Directly engaging to understand each other and work things out is an excellent first step. For this to work out well, each party must be willing to acknowledge their part of the conflict – what they did or did not do to cause it – and explore ways to mend the breach. Each person should reflect on their role, perhaps writing notes. This helps them decide how to proceed in addressing the conflict. The spiralling process can only be stopped with the right attitude, a genuine attempt to understand the true causes and adopting a collaborative approach to reverse the trend.

In determining a solution, it may also help to ask, "What can I realistically expect of the other party?" Making demands that the other person cannot meet sets you up for failure and undermines the relationship. In mediation, I often see people in conflict who have expectations that may be too demanding and unrealistic.

Even when the other party is willing to work things out, they may need help fulfilling all that is demanded of them because it is beyond their capacity. To maintain the relationship with them, determine beforehand what you want from the other individual and whether they can fulfil your requests. It honours them in the process. Asking for too much sets you up to further frustration and even failure.

Involve a mediator

Regrettably, direct personal engagement with someone you are in conflict with might only be possible sometimes, especially when emotions are out of control. So, if they do not listen to you, Jesus recommends that you bring someone else along. I recommend hiring a trained mediator where available to listen to both of you. They are great at helping people get to the bottom of the issue. But any other objective third party agreed on by both sides may be able to play this role.

Sometimes, you may need to skip straight to this step, especially where there are considerable power differences at play that make individual confrontation untenable, culturally inadvisable, or unsafe, such as a junior confronting a senior, a young girl confronting an older man, or a victim confronting someone who has used their power to hurt others before.

The mediator serves as both a witness and a neutral voice who can try to help you resolve the problems and move on. They are objective third parties who can help individuals engage with each other to agree on a common way forward. Again, at this point, if the

> **Think of a time when someone approached you as a third party when they were in a conflict. How did you help them repair the relationship or encourage them to seek closure?**
>
> ....
> ....
> ....
> ....
> ....

person works through the issues with you, then you have resolved the conflict. In the next chapter, we will provide a set of questions that a mediator may use to help bring clarity to a situation.

In the case study at the start of this chapter, Atwoli's son and brother decided they wanted to avoid a lawsuit if possible. Since they had already tried working with Mumbi directly, and she remained uncooperative, they involved a third party by approaching two elders who had been friends of Atwoli's for a very long time. They requested their help to talk to Mumbi to seek a joint agreement on Atwoli's burial.

At first, Mumbi was adamant that she was the rightful wife and did not need to cooperate with Atwoli's brother and son. However, the elders pleaded with her to cooperate, even assuring her that if she did, they and the other elders would advocate for her when it came time to discuss the inheritance of her late husband's properties, including the ancestral land in the village. Mumbi knew this would be the stickiest of the situations and didn't want to get a lawyer involved, so she agreed to the offer for the tribal members to mediate between her and Atwoli's other family.

She did, however, lay out several demands that she believed served her interests, including that she, as a Catholic, would be the one to determine the final rites for her husband's burial. This was a manageable condition for the family to work with. Their primary demand was that Atwoli be buried in the village's ancestral land, not the city cemetery. Although Mumbi did not like the prospect of having his grave so far from her children, the promise that she would get the area where he was buried as part of her inheritance was appealing. By agreeing to each other's demands, the elders helped the family avoid expensive court battles and give Atwoli a proper tribal burial. They also started the process of discussing inheritance rights within the family.

Seeking closure

However, suppose the offender does not listen to you or listen to the mediator you brought with you. In that case, Jesus recommends that you go to the community, in this case, probably a church or other community group. This aligns with many traditional African cultures, where involving mediators to address problems, resolve or transform conflict, and then go to the community is common practice.

If the person is unwilling to engage with the rest of the community, the community will ostracize that person in the hope that they will see sense and return to engage. Jesus agrees that if they do not listen to you, the mediator, or the community, you are free to dissociate with them and let them go. In a sense, you are free from the responsibility of making amends and transforming your relationship with them.

However, the goal is always to try to restore the relationship. Matthew 18 must be read in the context of Jesus's broader teachings for loving God and loving one another because our concern for others' welfare is fundamental. Still, the circumstances, especially the other party's cooperation, may sabotage that process, in which case Jesus recommends moving on.

Sometimes the relationship is not worth fighting for. Occasionally it is, but if the other person is unwilling to fight for it, you cannot fight alone. But if we have followed this process, we can walk away confident, knowing we did all we could to transform the relationship.

For example, I knew a woman who was trying to repair her relationship with her husband. Her husband had been unfaithful and even abusive. I don't recommend anyone stay in an abusive situation, and I believe that unfaithfulness is biblical grounds for divorce. We will talk more about abuse in another chapter.

But the wife went far above and beyond what was required or recommended. She did almost everything imaginable to try to save their marriage. She was forgiving and willing to take him back and even repair the relationship as much as possible. She worked with their pastor, consulted different counsellors and therapists, and even joined a marriage support group. She tried to be endearing to her husband, always inviting him to participate in counselling and the support group. He was not willing.

After several years, the wife finally ended their relationship through a formal divorce. Without the cooperation of her husband, she could only take the process so far. I am not, however, suggesting that victims of abuse or infidelity should follow her pattern; this is an extreme example meant to demonstrate that there are situations where maintaining the relationship is not within your power. Reconciliation may not be possible due to the other person's attitudes or unwillingness.

In that case, reframe your goal as closure for yourself and the relationship. This is the right approach to resolving these conflicts because you need to ensure that the other person does not continue to harm or exploit you. Although it may not have been your ideal way to resolve the conflict, closure is still a valid and necessary option for resolving a dispute.

Conclusion

When conflicts arise, clarify your goals in engaging the other person. To prepare, ask about the other party's commitment and cooperation. By gradually testing the other person's willingness to cooperate, you can determine how much effort to employ to resolve the conflict, what tactics to use, and whether the dispute can indeed be resolved. Of course, even where the other is not as committed, you can still apply yourself as part of "living at peace with all." In the next chapter, we discuss how to determine how much effort to put into fighting for the relationship versus a specific desired outcome.

Imagine you are invited to teach a local high-school group on the processes of determining how to think through a conflict situation and determine the pathways for engagement. Design your lesson below.

....
....
....
....
....
....
....
....
....
....

Group Discussion

1. How does your community support people in conflict situations? For example, do individuals play the role of a mediator, or are those in conflicts left alone to figure things out themselves? What would you like to see change in the way this is done?

2. Discuss a recent public conflict the group is familiar with and how that was handled. What helpful steps were followed? What steps were missed? What were the results? How could this have turned out differently?

5

Weigh the Relationship and the Issue

> *Thuol odonjo e koo* (LUO, WESTERN KENYA).
>
> "A snake has entered into the gourd.
> (How do you get it out without breaking the gourd?)"
> **MEANING:**
> There is trouble in the house. How do you get rid of the
> trouble without bringing down the whole house?

Mike and Juma met on the first day of high school and became fast friends. They played together on the school rugby team and were often in and out of each other's homes. At university, they continued being teammates as well as roommates. They both studied computer science. People called them "the brothers".

For their final college project, they developed an app to track vegetables from farm to customer, helping consumers distinguish contaminated vegetables from clean ones. The idea won first place in a national competition. They needed the start-up capital to launch the company and the app. But both came from poorer families, and few venture capitalists were willing to help.

Mike, a Christian, knew a friend at a local bank who was willing to introduce them to the loans manager. However, an unsecured loan would carry a heavier-than-usual interest rate of 24 per cent. Juma, who was from a strict Muslim family, objected. It was against his religion to borrow money, especially if they would have to pay interest to the bank. He could only borrow from friends or within the family, where he did not have to pay interest. But he needed someone to come up with the money they needed.

This threw the company's idea into a tailspin. Mike was disappointed, but cared about Juma and could not just cut him off and start the company alone. Juma considered the opportunity important, but so was his religious faith. Both were worried that their relationship of more than 10 years would end because of a business idea.

They resolved to shelve the idea, take jobs in the industry, and save to raise some capital. But, given the poor job market, they could only land jobs for a few months at a time. Mike told Juma one day, "We can't sit on this idea for much longer. Someone else will get the same idea, and all our hard work will be for nothing. You need to loosen up a bit, bro. Otherwise, I might be forced to go ahead without you. There's no other way."

Juma retorted, "Are you threatening me now? I can't believe that, after all we've been through, all you can think about is money. Does our friendship mean nothing to you?"

"Of course, you're my friend, man. But should your religion stop me from eating?"

"So, what do you want me to do?"

The previous chapter discussed determining the process to follow when you face a conflict by asking, "How open is the other party to cooperation?" This is important if you want to develop your conflict competence and protect your relationships. This chapter helps you ask the following question: "How important is the issue compared to the relationship?" Depending on the answer, there are six approaches to resolving the conflict effectively.

How Important Is the Issue Compared to the Relationship?

The second set of questions is:

- How important is the issue compared to the relationship?
  - ○ How much do I value this relationship? What am I willing to invest or sacrifice to keep the relationship?
  - ○ How important is my view or desired outcome? What am I willing to invest or sacrifice to get what I want?
  - ○ Am I standing up for my view and rights, or is this a matter of principle, justice, or defending someone else?

This second set of questions helps you decide how much effort, time, and other resources to invest in transforming the relationship. Different ways of engaging in conflict have additional costs. By cost, I don't only mean money, although that might be part of it, but also emotional costs, time, effort, and relational damage. You may sacrifice time and effort to seek a solution for a highly collaborative process. In a win-lose solution, one side may sacrifice more of their desired outcome while the other may sacrifice goodwill. Most of the chapters in this book focus on situations where both people value the relationship and are able to collaborate toward conflict transformation.

How you approach a conflict often depends on how much each party values the relationship compared to the issue. To illustrate this, I've developed a revised version of the Thomas-Kilmann Conflict Mode Inventory, the internationally recognized model we encountered in an earlier chapter. I use the quadrants developed under the TKI to highlight how you may want to proceed when in a conflict situation.[1]

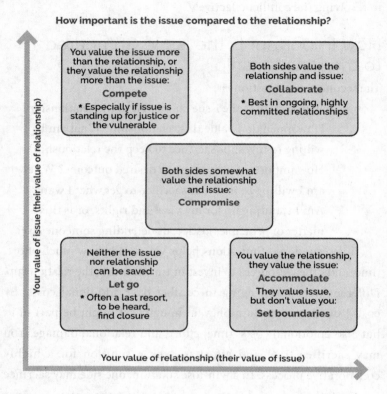

How important is the issue compared to the relationship?

Your value of issue (their value of relationship)

You value the issue more than the relationship, or they value the relationship more than the issue:
Compete
* Especially if issue is standing up for justice or the vulnerable

Both sides value the relationship and issue:
Collaborate
* Best in ongoing, highly committed relationships

Both sides somewhat value the relationship and issue:
Compromise

Neither the issue nor relationship can be saved:
Let go
* Often a last resort, to be heard, find closure

You value the relationship, they value the issue:
Accommodate
They value issue, but don't value you:
Set boundaries

Your value of relationship (their value of issue)

A previous chapter explained how the TKI describes the five different approaches to conflict that people tend to take. Although we tend to get stuck in our default approaches to conflict, each approach is important within a specific context. A problem arises when we use our dominant approach in situations where other approaches would be more effective or appropriate. When you are

---

1 Some content in this chapter about the TKI is adapted from: "The Thomas Kilmann Conflict Mode Instrument Test (TKI Test)," Career Assessment Site, accessed April 17, 2023, https://careerassessmentsite.com/tests/thomas-kilmann-tki-tests/about-the-thomas-kilmann-conflict-mode-instrument-tki/.

entering into a conflict transformation process, it is helpful to determine your goal, and that will in turn influence the approach you take.

The y-axis (up and down) is usually about your own assertiveness. Since we should be more assertive when we value the issue highly, I've called that your value of the issue. I have changed the x-axis (left and right), which is usually about your cooperativeness, to show that we are more cooperative when we highly value the relationship.

The revised chart shows how each party's value of the relationship versus the issue will lead to different approaches to the conflict. For instance, if both parties highly value the relationship and highly value the issue, they will be more willing to take the time and energy required to collaborate towards a mutually beneficial solution. If one person values the relationship while the other values the outcome of the issue, it will likely be a situation of the person who values the relationship having to accommodate the other person and the other person competing for or standing up for their view.

Collaborate

In the last chapter, we talked about how meaningful relationships are, how central they are to God's heart, and how preserving relationships in the long term is worth it. We described how to commit to the relationship, invest in it over time, and clarify a conflict engagement process. But even if you don't have a chance to do any of these, you can ask yourself at the beginning of a conflict: "Do we both value this relationship?"

If you affirm that preserving the relationship is vital to both of you, you can pursue a collaborative solution. You have already built goodwill by being friends, which is helpful for you when dealing with difficult circumstances, and trust each other enough to want to work together to address whatever issue you face. If you are both willing to take the time and put in the energy required, you can often find a mutually beneficial resolution. Collaboration offers us an opportunity for creative engagement in order to process the issues we face toward understanding. This is often the ideal situation for conflict transformation.

A family friend recently had to navigate some land succession issues. He grew up in a polygamous family. When the dad died, the elder wife and her sons tried to influence the succession process so the younger wife's family would be disadvantaged. They bribed the local administrators to declare them the only true successors. The younger wife's children were ready for a fight.

However, my friend, the firstborn son of the younger wife, reached out to the firstborn of the first wife. He understood that a fight would drain both families' few resources and, although this would be a quick win, there would be terrible long-term consequences. Initially, the half-brother was reluctant, so my friend sent him a letter explaining that he was committed to a peaceful and out-of-court resolution and that he did not want to see their families end up as enemies.

After three months without a response, my friend tried again to reach out through an intermediary, a village elder who knew the families well. The half-brother agreed to meet. Together, they decided to convince the family of their plan for resolution. Some members on both sides resisted, but they were all won over by the insistence of the two half-brothers, who were now working together as a team. As they promoted the plan to the rest of the family, they warned against the dangers of a continued conflict. More village elders got involved and helped the family process the succession out of court.

This process saved the family a considerable amount in legal fees, not to mention protecting their time and preventing untold animosity among family members. It all became a reality because there was a goal to rally everyone around. Trust was rebuilt in the family, and they remained friends.

Because my friend valued the relationship and got his half-brother to appreciate the value of the relationship as well, they were able to convince the rest of their families. He was committed to solving the problem of succession through a non-conflictual process. He determined from the beginning that his goal was to collaborate.

Compromise

A collaborative solution, while it leads to the best outcomes, also requires a lot of time and energy. If both parties value the relationship and the issue to some extent, they might make slightly less effort and find a compromise, each sacrificing some of their goals.

A compromise, especially in day-to-day situations, helps us keep moving forward in what can otherwise be an overwhelming number of daily decisions. For example, you and a friend need lunch. You have differing views on where you should go, especially if you are the one paying. You decide to go with one person's choice one day and agree that you will go to a different place on another day.

Or think of weightier decisions. You, as a family, are trying to decide where your children should attend school. Do you send them to a private school or a local public school? Suppose the father prefers a private school while the mother prefers a public school. This might lead to tension in the family. A joint decision is preferable, but sometimes this is difficult, leaving it to one of the parties to make the decision – hopefully, with the agreement of the other. This involves a compromise because you cannot go with both options.

If one person decided and the other accepted, that would be accommodation. For it to be a mutual compromise, each person is required to give and take. Perhaps the person who didn't get their

What are the differences between collaborating, compromising, and accommodating? How have you seen these three confused?

....

....

....

....

choice of public or private would get to select the specific school for the children. Maybe if they chose the private school, as the father wanted, he would find another way to finance that decision. Perhaps if they chose the public school, as the mother wanted, she would give the father the choice of who would tutor their children for the exams. Neither person would get exactly what they wanted, but they would each be able to address some of their concerns.

Accommodate

Sometimes, you may determine that the issue is of more importance to the other person than it is to you, whereas your priority is the relationship. In these situations, you may choose to accommodate their wishes.

For instance, Genesis 13 talks about how the workers of Abraham and his nephew Lot had gotten into a conflict over grazing land for their growing herds. In the Meru culture, there is a saying that "he who has a goat has goat problems". God was blessing them by increasing their livestock holdings – and the blessing came with responsibilities. The grazing land could not bear their flocks as well as people, so they needed to part ways.

It is how Abraham approaches this situation that is most interesting to me. Being a Near Eastern culture, you would have expected the elder to be the first to choose what he wanted and where to go. Similarly, among many African communities, the elders get to eat first. They get to choose the best seat, and they get to decide when there is a disagreement.

But Abraham displays his maturity and trust in God by allowing Lot to choose the land he wants for his livestock. Like all of us, Lot chooses with his own best benefits in mind. He goes to the valley because there is more grass and water for his animals there. This was the best of the two choices. We do not have a complete story here, but we do not read of Abraham complaining. He accepts Lot's choice and moves on to take the remaining part.

We know, however, that Lot's selfish choice becomes a problem because it puts him close to the sinful cities of Sodom and Gomorrah, and that Abraham is forced to rescue him afterward. Like Lot, I would have chosen the most suitable option too. But Lot may not have considered the risks of positioning himself closer to sin and how this would become a problem for his family and business. Eventually, he loses both and barely escapes with his life.

Abraham, on the other hand, prioritized maintaining a peaceful relationship with his nephew above gaining the best resources. He wanted to hang on to this relationship for the long term because Lot was family. Giving Lot the first choice was like Paul's encouragement to consider others better than ourselves (Philippians 2:3). This is not easy because we are all selfish at heart, consider our own needs first, and even desire the best for ourselves. But when we, like Abraham, depend on God in faith to provide for us, we can open our hands and hold lightly our desires, resources, and even our rights.

Accommodating should not be forced, or the person whose needs are overlooked can become resentful, which can further fuel

> **?**
>
> **What are some boundaries you have set in relationships?**
>
> ....
> ....
> ....
> ....
> ....

conflict. However, when done willingly, accommodating can be a humble and selfless choice to put others' needs first and prioritize harmony in a relationship.

Set Boundaries

It is interesting to note Abraham's choice to accommodate, especially as he had more power in the situation. If the power dynamic is unequal, there is often pressure for the person with less power to accommodate the more powerful individual. Differences in power could be due to social status, such as someone having more money, being from a dominant group, occupying a position of authority, or having a more forceful personality. The person who cares less about the relationship often also holds more power. When someone feels pressure to accommodate, they may be in a situation where they need to set boundaries instead. Identifying a misuse of power or when to stand up for yourself is an important skill to develop. It's often helpful when the other person doesn't value the relationship, and you value yourself.

When our kids were younger, my wife and I trained them to address disagreements with their friends through active conversations.

By *active*, we meant they should address the issue rather than walk away. Our emphasis was to help them discuss their interests, positions, and wants in any situation. We encouraged them to step back and say, "Let me think about that," or, "I sense that there is no fairness here. Can we talk about this?" We were trying to help them understand that many situations in life – even playing with friends – require setting ground rules for engagement. My kids needed to learn that they would sometimes need to deal with stronger people who would be tempted to leverage the circumstances to their advantage.

For example, one of my sons played basketball with a neighbourhood friend outside our house. My son was getting frustrated, complaining that the friend, who was bigger and taller than he, was using his body in a way that made it difficult for them to play evenly. He was pushing and being aggressive in ways not acceptable in a friendly game.

Eventually, my son stopped the game. He held his ball, inviting a conversation with his friend. His friend subsequently changed how he played. I was proud that my son did not become aggressive, yell, or call his friend names. Instead, he clearly stated what he needed for play to continue. By withdrawing support for the aggressive behaviour and engaging in a conversation, the two re-established some ground rules and could continue playing.

Some people intend to harm you because of negative influences in their own lives. I remember a neighbour who had a boundary dispute with our family. Even though he had a bigger portion of land, he still wanted to gain a tiny sliver more. That seemed to him to be substantial enough that he would throw away relationships with us as his neighbours. It wasn't until we had an official demarcation done on the pieces of land that we saw that he had extended the boundaries to take advantage of us. Influenced by greed, he had gone to significant lengths to gain the upper hand.

In this situation, we had to re-set the boundaries that our neighbour had overstepped – and continue to enforce them whenever he tried to encroach again. This image illustrates other, less visible boundaries we need to set and maintain for the sake of healthy relationships with our neighbours.

Of course, a kids' basketball game is one thing, but a relationship with an abusive boss with the power to fire you is very different. Setting boundaries is appropriate when you still have some power to call a timeout, but when a situation turns out to be abusive, you may be unable to stop the aggression. In those extremes, I taught my kids to identify when the other person was taking advantage of them and to either walk away from the situation or report the matter to someone in authority. Now that they are adults, I can look back and identify when they withdrew or wisely decided to let go to protect themselves from further harm. In a later chapter, we will discuss how to spot and respond to abusive behaviour.

Compete or Fight

If winning the argument is more important than sustaining the relationship, one will typically compete to get one's way. Most of the time, we must guard against the temptation to compete to gain an advantage. We are all familiar with people interested in winning arguments at all costs. These individuals would rather be right than foster better understanding and work out relationships with others. Do you remember how it felt when someone walked all over you? That person may have argued their way into what they considered a win and care little about your feelings or your ongoing relationship with them. Since we've all experienced this terrible behaviour, maybe we should consider it a suitable warning for us not to do the same when dealing with others.

We need to consciously guard against short-term goals, like winning the argument of the moment or overpowering the opponent so that they give in to our views or positions. Profound and long-lasting relationships must include caring about the needs of the other.

Although we should not compete to overpower others to get our way, there are situations where we should fight for our position. The difference is when our position is not about our advantage or rights but rather about a principle, defending the vulnerable, or justice. While the TKI assessment often warns against competing, I include it here as a valid approach but call it "fighting", with the understanding that you are fighting for a principle or for others.

Sometimes, the conflict is simply about a principle, and you may need to take a stand because, although not resolving the issue, that is the most honourable position. In an abusive relationship, you can separate from or hold off on a relationship in order to protect yourself. In other circumstances, you need to stand up for what is right, even if that creates disharmony.

In Acts 15:36-41, we read about Paul and Barnabas, who were close missionary colleagues and travelled together, preaching and teaching in Asia Minor and Europe. As is the case for itinerant ministers, they tended to pick up support staff or colleagues as they moved about. At some point, John Mark joined them in their travel and ministry. But on their journey to Pamphylia, Mark deserted them. This, of course, riled Paul.

When Barnabas suggested they take Mark along on the next journey, Paul did not think that wise. This led to such a fierce disagreement that the two chose other partners and parted company, travelling to different ministry destinations.

We don't have much detail about the conflict, so many questions have been raised about these two "super" Christians and why they reacted so unexpectedly. Why couldn't they find common ground, maybe bring in Mark but admonish him, or have him prove himself on the next trip?

One can argue that, in this case, Paul was standing up against Barnabas on principle and vice versa. For Paul, the ministry the two were involved in was essential and sometimes risky. You could not afford to have half-hearted colleagues on the team. To do so would compromise the ministry and even endanger others. Mark's desertion at Pamphylia, which seems abrupt (maybe even unapproved by the other team members), terribly disappointed Paul.

For Barnabas, however, the principle of denying Mark from coming along for ministry was wrong. Mark deserved another chance and should be included in the team. Barnabas may have argued that bringing him back would be an excellent way to train or mentor him to be a more trustworthy companion. Whatever the argument, from either side, we know that they disagreed bitterly to the point of going separate ways.

One wonders why Luke, the author, included this incident in his writings. It must have significantly impacted him and the rest of the team. We learn that sometimes we need to stand on principle and walk away if those principles are compromised or threatened. Or, we may have to defend a relationship out of principle, even when the other party has taken advantage of us. In either case, the choice must be well thought out in engagement with the other party.

Sometimes, you take different positions and go in different directions because of principles that each party recognizes as vital for them. The warning here is to do all you can to be open about your position and available to change where necessary. Even if you eventually disagree, you can still affirm the relationship with mutual respect and ensure you do not burn relational bridges.

We read later that Paul did not hold a grudge against Mark for the rest of his life – a temptation we encounter often. In later writings, Paul expresses deep respect for Mark (Colossians 4:10). He writes to Timothy, "Bring Mark with you when you come, for he will be helpful to me in my ministry" (2 Timothy 4:11). Finally, we also see that Mark supported Paul during his imprisonment in Rome (Philemon 23-24), which indicates that their relationship was restored. We can assume that part of this was because Paul's cutting off Mark from an earlier engagement was purely on principle and not on personality.

Sometimes, standing up for a principle means pursuing justice. The victim may go to the offender to seek payment for the damage caused. This is a noble goal that more of us need to pursue rather than holding a grudge and walking away. On the other hand, the perpetrator must also be willing to provide the appropriate repayments to repair the damage.

Withdraw, Let Go, Forgive

There is another approach that the TKI calls "Avoiding" when it is used as a default style of approaching conflict. People withdraw, disengage, refuse to discuss issues, and write off the other party when they disagree. When it is overused as the default approach to conflict, it demonstrates a low commitment to relationships.

However, when a conflict occurs and neither side values either the relationship or the issue very highly, it is unlikely they will put much energy into resolving the dispute. Relationships grow only if the parties are equally committed to each other.

You may have tried to develop a relationship with someone, but they put very little effort into the process. You call them, but they never call you – and not just because they don't like talking on the phone! In these cases, how well does the relationship develop? It doesn't make a difference no matter how hard you try in these unbalanced relationships. The other person is simply not committed.

Now consider what this would look like in a conflict situation. Perhaps you have repeatedly set boundaries, but the person continues to overstep them. This reaches a point where maintaining the relationship is more harmful than beneficial, and your self-preservation must become a priority. The other person is clearly not invested in the relationship and is unwilling to cooperate, so it is best for you to disengage.

Another example is when someone has significantly broken your trust and is unrepentant. My friend in the US had a cousin who invited him to invest in a project to charter several boats on Lake Victoria to ferry tourists on a day trip to an infamous island. The dictator Idi Amin had exiled some of his opponents to this island and killed them there. The cousin assured my friend they could make money running these day trips for tourists.

My friend blindly entered the business because it sounded like a great idea. He should have asked for a clear business plan or a formal agreement. Indeed, months later, when he tried to collect his portion of the profits, the cousin evaded him. After talking to other family members, he realized that the business did not exist. The fraudster cousin had been dishonest from the start, only wanting to lay hands on some quick cash.

Honesty and openness are the foundations of good relationships. Sometimes, we decide to withhold information or not be fully honest with people because we fear they will take advantage of us. Without trust, our relationships remain superficial. But the depth and intimacy we crave can only be found when we open up and commit. While relationships have different degrees of commitment and intimacy, intentionally withholding information, limiting interactions, and being coldly formal signify an unbalanced relationship. It either needs to die or is ripe for transformation through honest confrontation.

Once you realize that you cannot get what you want out of a disagreement (the issue), and the relationship can no longer be maintained, withdrawing may be the best route. We already discussed this in the extreme case described in Matthew 18, where the person is unwilling to cooperate, despite the mediator and the community's involvement.

In these cases, you may change your goal for how to transform the conflict. Your new plan may simply be to have the other person hear you and acknowledge the hurt and pain caused. Even though the relationship is not likely to continue, you can still communicate the injury and, maybe, be understood.

I remember, for example, mediating between neighbours in an apartment complex. The woman only wanted to be understood and was not seeking a continued relationship with the man next door. She just wanted her neighbour to know that what he had said about her son had offended her.

Fortunately, her neighbour understood the harm he had caused, apologized, and made amends. This helped their living situation. They would never be best buddies, but at least no one held a grudge. But this may not always be the case. Sometimes, you may convey your message to the other person and not receive the expected response.

While avoiding – as the TKI describes it – can be passive, I am advocating for a process of letting go that requires hard work. Conflicts may begin as simple disagreements and differences, but they can escalate to real hurts and sin against each other – especially when you consider withdrawing. In these situations, apology and forgiveness will be needed to resolve the conflict, whether the relationship continues or not.

Although forgiveness is vital in repairing relationships, it must never be demanded as a condition to continue the relationship.

Apologies and forgiveness must always be given and received willingly and in no way be used to gain the upper hand in a relationship.

To restore a relationship, people may also need to make amends and compensate for the hurt caused. Sometimes, pursuing justice means pursuing these repayments even when the other person does not freely offer them. Sometimes, however, it may be wiser to simply forgive and let go.

We draw strength for this from Jesus's teachings about forgiveness, love for enemies, and treatment of those who mistreat us. Indeed, Jesus is the perfect model of how we should live in peace with all others. In his teachings and his life, he shows the ideals of loving God and loving other people, as well as forgiving others when they hurt us. We will speak more about this in another chapter.

Wisdom and Discernment

We live in societies that offer differing models for reacting to conflict, including revenge and getting even. It takes courage to reject these and to de-escalate rather than react in anger. It takes conviction to seek peace rather than harming the other and to pursue the approaches I propose here. It takes discernment and wisdom to choose an alternative process.

Courage tells us it is best to work for peace rather than the alternative. It takes foresight to invest in the lifespan of a relationship rather than just opt for the immediate and the expedient. You may live determined to find alternatives likely to lead to win-win solutions, even if there are short-term losses and compromises. Win-win efforts help build trust, which is the bedrock of long-term relationships.

These decisions are very personal, but seeking advice from others may well help determine the best way possible. However, remember that people who do not share similar convictions may not understand why you would make certain decisions – like not pursuing your "rights", forgiving, or not seeking revenge or retribution. Seeking to repair the relationship and seeking help from mediators are alternatives that many may not subscribe to. Wisdom is vital to discern what is worth fighting for.

Conclusion

Mike and Juma sat down to evaluate their goals. The last thing they wanted was to lose their friendship, have one person profit from the idea alone, create competitive businesses later, or start suing each other over ideas. They needed to find a middle ground to honour their efforts, maintain their divergent religious principles, and preserve their relationship. They were both willing to collaborate.

Eventually, they came to a resolution that felt good for both. Mike, who identified as a Christian, would form the company under his name. He would borrow the money and hire Juma as a contractor. Juma would also reserve the right to buy up to 40 per cent of the company shares whenever he chooses. Mike and Juma formalized their agreement and how they would interact by signing a contract.

In this chapter, I reviewed a set of questions that encourages considering the goals for the relationship and, therefore, the efforts required to transform a conflict. How vital is the issue compared to the relationship? There are many goals to consider, including asserting one's position when necessary or embracing a mutual benefit that means working together for change. It requires effort and wisdom to know when and how to engage.

In the next chapter, I introduce the concept of distinguishing between the person you are in conflict with and the issues you may be fighting over. People are not the problem, even though society may argue that they are. The problem is the problem!

Revisit your TKI results. What is the most common way you react to conflicts in your relationships? Why do you think this is the case? What areas do you need to focus on developing to ensure healthy relationships?

....
....
....
....
....
....
....
....
....
....
....

Group Discussion

1. Take turns to share your TKI assessment results with your group. If you feel comfortable, ask the group to comment on your results. Keep it positive, please!

2. Reflect on the biblical stories mentioned in this chapter, such as Abraham and Lot or Paul and Barnabas. What was surprising to you about their conflicts? How would you have responded if you were in their situations?

The Problem
Is the Problem

It was a warm afternoon at Sunny Solar, a Chinese company recently established in the southwest district. Muruku, the operations manager, called Remi into his office. Remi was disturbed because the operations manager only talked to staff to promote or fire them. Remi was not doing well in the company and suspected he was being fired.

Remi's mind raced back and forth as he sat in the open waiting area of Muruku's office. He had been in the job for only nine months, but had already been written up twice for alleged non-performance. He needed this job. He and his wife had just had a baby, and his wife was not working. His manager, Jelani, did not seem to like him.

That must be why she had reported him to the ops manager again, thought Remi. Muruku would probably believe Jelani's account because they were from the same tribe. There was a rumour among the other workers that the two were related, which was why Jelani had been made a manager.

"Come on in," Muruku said. Remi rose and slowly stepped into Muruku's office, trying to block his negative thoughts. He was shaken, but also ready to fight. "Remi, you know why I called you into my office?" Muruku said, without looking at him.

"Jelani?"

"Why Jelani?" Muruku thundered. "You think I would call you into my office to discuss your manager? You think I have that much time on my hands?"

"No, sir."

"Remi, I called you here because your production numbers are terrible. You are not keeping up with our standards. We hire people and keep them here only if they can produce. Do you understand?"

"Yes, sir," Remi replied quietly.

"Do you understand?" Muruku shouted again, as if to drive an arrow deeper into a dying animal.

"Look, Jelani does not like me," Remi started to respond with a quivering voice. "I know that because, when I started here, she gave me a higher quota to fill than the others and did not give me good training. I feel overwhelmed. I cannot meet these quotas because they are beyond my abilities . . ."

"So, you are telling me you are incapable? Then why should I have you working here? Look, if you want this job, I need this record to change, and in the next 14 days. Plus, I do not want to hear that nonsense about Jelani hating you. I do not want to hear about it if you don't have the guts to talk over things with her. That is business between the two of you. All right? All I want is for these numbers to be up. Last warning! Okay?"

"Okay."

"I will personally review these in two weeks, and if they are not up, you are gone. You are free to go," Muruku said, showing Remi the door.

Remi walked out quietly. He did not know whether to say thank-you or not.

Once outside the office, walking back to the production floor, Remi felt a wave of anger flood through him. He wished he could have defended himself better. He had felt tongue-tied as the manager threatened. He also felt Jelani should have talked to him before reporting him to the manager.

Remi went straight to his line and resumed work, fitting pieces into solar panels before final assembly. But his heart was still beating fast, and his mind could not focus.

"Remi," called co-worker Tati. "What did you go to do in the ops manager's office? Don't tell me you are being promoted after only a few months on the job!"

Remi just stared at Tati.

Tati got the message; this was not a joking matter. "I am sorry, my friend, I didn't mean to pry. I hope all is well."

"It's okay," Remi replied flatly, turning around to focus on his work.

People and Points

Every misunderstanding is about an issue in relation to another person. In other words, conflict is about people, but it is also about points. At the heart of every conflict is an issue the parties are trying to navigate, and these issues may be related to different interests, positions, or even personalities.

If the issue is not addressed and the conflict grows, there is a possibility that the parties in conflict begin to see *each other* as the problem rather than the issue. We may begin to see the other person as the enemy and therefore consider them the opposition and even attack them. It takes a lot of effort to keep the focus on the issue and maintain objectivity, especially when in an emotional conflict.

For true conflict transformation, it is important to address the issues that caused the conflict and, as much as possible, not simply blame the other person. The problem is the problem, not the person. This attitude shift isn't always easy to adopt, but it has profound potential to get you out of conflict and preserve your relationships. Indeed, there is little hope of getting out of a conflict unless you can address the underlying issue at its source!

Personality, Points of View, and Perceptions

It is easy to see where the confusion between people and problems comes in when we consider that differences often contribute to conflicts.

Conflict can arise simply because of a difference in personalities. Our *personality* includes our unique emotional patterns of thinking, feeling, and behaving. Everyone's personality is as unique as their thumbprint, but there are broad categories of classifying *personalities*. For instance, introverted people prefer to protect their personal space, while extroverted people are energized by relating with others, as I mentioned in a previous chapter about my late wife and me.

Our different *points of view* – how we see the world – can affect conflict too. Our point of view can come from having a different opinion, access to certain information, ignorance, an intuitive nature, personal interpretations, or even bias. Points of view can change with circumstances and differ even among close friends and family. Some people, for instance, see the glass as half full, while others see the glass as half empty. Observing the same circumstances, an optimist may see the good, and a pessimist may see what is wrong.

Many conflicts are related to differences in perceptions – in other words, our beliefs and interpretations of reality. We all perceive things differently. You can interview people who observed a similar occurrence and came to different conclusions about what they witnessed. For example, my friend and her four male colleagues were recruiting a new employee. The men were excited to hire a particular female applicant. However, my friend was uncomfortable with the appointment. When pushed to explain her hesitation, she could only say that she did not feel the new hire was the right person for the team. As a result, the team was deadlocked.

Our differences should not be mistaken for the root issue of why we are in a conflict. An extroverted or introverted personality is not the problem – in fact, they can complement each other well, as my wife and I did. The real issue is what we choose to do with the circumstances we face and how we manage the problem. We can overcome these by treating them as just that, differences, and not as determinants of conflicts.

In the hiring scenario outlined above, the team leader did more background checks and called at least two references from the candidate's previous workplace. It turned out that my friend's fears were valid. Others had apparently found it challenging to work with the applicant and mentioned concerns about her character, which was why she was looking for a different job. My friend's intuition this saved the team from hiring a potentially problematic employee.

So, while differences between logical and intuitive perception styles had initially caused a conflict on the team, they had led to a better solution. They highlighted the real issue: needing more information about the candidate. To avoid confusing the issue with personal differences, it is essential to cultivate awareness of yourself and others. What are your personalities? What may be influencing each of your points of view? What are your differing perceptions of the issue? Clarifying these can help understand why you may have different approaches and thus identify the real issue.

Are Identities the Problem?

Another difference frequently cited as the problem is differing identities. In the case study outlined in this chapter's opening, it is easy to imagine Remi's side of the story – that the issue is probably about ethnic rivalry and interpersonal hatred.

Of course, ethnic identities – and any of our identities – are not a problem in and of themselves. We are created with a need for connection with others. Even for the most introverted individuals, human relations remain a crucial part of our being. We are born into a family, and through socialization, we are nurtured to identify and relate first with those in our family and community – our in-group. Our in-group teaches us much about how to relate and deal with others in the broader community – the out-group.

Self-understanding includes discovering how we are wired and how we were trained to relate with others – both the in- and out-groups. What are our views of outsiders or people who are different from us? What were we taught about people of a different gender, of different ages (younger or older), or from other communities (tribes, regions, nations, etc.)? Most of this training is healthy and helps us easily navigate relations with others.

However, some of those learned behaviours come with negative baggage that makes relationships difficult. That includes stereotypes or cookie-cutter generalizations of other people, their characteristics, and behaviours. For example, you may have heard statements like, "the people from that tribe/region are [fill in the blank]." Or "men/women are [fill in the blank]." Most of these statements, passed around liberally in conversations within the in-group, are harmful, untrue, and often demeaning to the other group.

Have you held a stereotype about a group, only to find out when you made a friend from that group that you had been wrong all along? Perhaps you met someone from another tribe and discovered that the stories you heard growing up did not align with what your new friend was like. In Kenya, many age-old stereotypes were hyped up and exploited, first by colonial powers and then by political opportunists to divide and rule the common people. Unfortunately, these beliefs impact how we relate to people who hold those identities.

As a result, identities become cast as the problem when, in reality, it is the assumptions, labels, and stereotypes that negatively colour our interpretation of situations in conflict. In conflicts, when we hold differing opinions or if I dislike you for whatever reasons (your personality, background, or experience, for example), I might choose to interpret whatever you say in a biased way – leading to a misinterpretation of your message or motives. In this case, it is not so much the message or the medium of communication but what I choose to hear. Because of the stereotypes I hold, I can more easily create an enemy out of you, causing walls to go up or gears to lock.

Write down some stereotypes of other groups that you were taught while growing up or have heard about others and your own group. How do these stereotypes affect how different groups relate in your community/country?

. . . .

. . . .

. . . .

. . . .

This is a painful experience for the person being stereotyped or blamed. Remember the last time this happened to you? It may be something you said or did that the other individual understood quite differently. They then questioned your intentions and your character. Maybe it was no more than a poor choice of words on your part, but a misunderstanding arose. You felt ashamed that you were careless or had not thought through your words or actions.

But instead of the other person focusing on the misunderstanding, some part of your identity was suddenly under attack. It was no longer about what you did, but who you are. At that point, your priority changed. You weren't going to apologize when told you are a terrible person. They had gone too far, and admitting your fault would only prove their stereotype right. You needed to defend yourself! Blaming and unjustified personal attacks cause defensive responses.

This is one way we begin to focus on the other as the problem rather than on the issues between us. We may be tempted to assume the very worst of the motives and intentions of others and regard them with ill will. We may also stew over their evil against us. We become bitter and even revengeful. Unfortunately, this strategy only digs us deeper into the ruts of anger and despondency. Sometimes, the other may feel the need to defend themselves or react similarly, which only heightens the stakes. Suppose I see myself as better than someone else, and they do the same. In that case, no one will have the humility to acknowledge their responsibility or address the issues together, leading to a lose-lose situation.

Unless there is an intentional decision to step back or to stop digging ourselves deeper into the conflict, our communication becomes dedicated to defending ourselves, making things worse. We are in danger of allowing the conflict to grow beyond the initial causes and spiralling out of control.

What about Discrimination?

But what about when discrimination is at play? Sometimes, people's identities do affect the issue at hand.

We find a clear example of this in the biblical story in the book of Acts (Acts 6). A conflict arises in Jerusalem between the Hellenistic and Hebraic Jewish believers over the care for widows overlooked in the daily food distributions. The Hebraic Jews grew up in Israel, spoke Aramaic and/or Hebrew, and stuck closely to Jewish customs. Jesus, and probably most of his disciples, were Hebraic Jews. The Hellenistic Jews came from other parts of the Roman Empire, spoke Greek, and were more influenced by the Greek worldview. These groups did not worship in the same synagogues, but as people from both groups began to follow Jesus, they found themselves in similar fellowships.

We do not have the details, but there seems to have been some discrimination against the Hellenists in the way food was distributed to widows in the early church. One part of the issue was resource allocation and possibly misallocation. Another part was the mistreatment of one group by another. That stemmed from an interethnic conflict with a possible basis in the backgrounds and traditions of these two groups.

The apostles intervened to wisely address both issues. They did not criticize or label any of the groups. Instead, they devised a process to address the issue. They appointed deacons known for their integrity and fairness to oversee the food distribution, and the apostles continued to preach and teach. This solved the problem without weighing down the entire fellowship or distracting the apostles from teaching the scriptures. But, importantly, all the deacons who were appointed had Greek names. In other words, the apostles chose leaders from the Hellenistic community, which was being overlooked, to ensure that community's concerns were addressed. The issue was not only inequities in food distribution, but also perceived or actual discrimination. The apostles' solution addressed both concerns.

The solution, therefore, demonstrated that shifting the focus to the issue instead of the person does not mean being blind to how people's identities affect the situation. The Hebraic Jews appear to have had more power in this scenario, so the apostles gave more power to the Hellenistic Jews. They recognized that these were not just identities but power dynamics. Until the power dynamic was balanced, it would be difficult for people to focus on the real issue.

You have likely encountered other scenarios where someone's identity affected the power dynamic, making it challenging to apply conflict resolution techniques.

For instance, although it is changing, old age is synonymous with wisdom in many traditional African (and Asian and Latin) communities. You may not be considered an adult until well into your 40s, and even then, you are required to listen and not talk when in the company of older folk, especially men. You may have great ideas and even be more learned than the elders, but your views are not readily invited. These power differences manifest strongly when an elder conflicts with a younger person. The assumption is that the younger person will acquiesce to the elder's demands, even when they are wrong. People cannot focus on the issue, because anyone who disagrees with the elder risks being accused of disrespect, making the person the problem. This presents untold opportunities for abuse. The same could be said for women left out of such communities' discussions.

However, power differences can be overcome if both sides come to the table with the desire to address the issues openly with a wish to move forward. For example, a boss and subordinate relationship can have some power differences that, because the boss can fire the subordinate, may make it difficult to engage in a conflict situation from an equal footing. Without a safe space provided by the boss, the subordinate may risk retaliation or walk away in fear. However, if the boss is open-minded, and wants to learn, the possibility for a better resolution to a conflict is multiplied.

Focusing on the issues as the core problem helps you treat the other person as human and as an individual with dignity. They are not just a stereotype, even when they share the identities of a particular group or community. Understanding this reduces the possibility of creating an "us versus them" scenario and focuses instead on how to solve the issues that might have led to the current situation.

Adam, Eve, and the Blame Game

In one way or another, all the problems we face today can be traced back to one important conflict when the first humans refused to take responsibility for the issue and chose to blame others instead.

In the Garden of Eden, the first man and woman experienced harmony, a peaceful co-existence in a perfect creation under God. But sin destroyed all that with the first conflict. When they chose to eat the fruit God had told them not to eat, God confronted them.

Rather than take responsibility, they immediately became selfish and blamed everyone but themselves. Adam blamed his once-perfect wife and indirectly blamed God: "It was the woman you gave me who gave me the fruit, and I ate it" (Genesis 3:12).

But the person – Eve – was not the problem. In fact, she had been the solution to his earlier problem of loneliness! When God brought the woman to the man for the first time, Adam (the man) was thrilled: "At last . . . This one is bone from my bone, and flesh from my flesh! She will be called 'woman', because she was taken from 'man'" (Genesis 2:23).

By saying "The woman you gave me", Adam also implied that it was God's fault for putting her there in the first place. Was he suggesting that he would not have sinned if Eve were not there?

The woman, in turn, blamed the serpent: "The serpent deceived me . . . That's why I ate it" (Genesis 3:13). The serpent was part of God's creation given to Eve to steward and rule over. Was Eve saying she forgot God's instructions not to eat from the tree?

Both Adam and Eve condemn others as the problem instead of focusing on the issue – their choice to disobey. We know God was clear in his instructions for acting in the garden. Even though the serpent cast doubt, insinuating both a miscommunication and bad faith on the side of God, God's instructions were well-defined and Adam and Eve knew what God had said. The real issue was the temptation to "be like God" that they could not resist. Adam and Eve chose to misconstrue God's instructions to be like God for their own selfish desires – but they did not want to admit it.

In choosing to pass the blame, Adam and Eve built walls of deception around themselves and against themselves and God. They refused to face the central issues of their condition, own up to their disobedience, or take responsibility for their sins. Instead, they skirted the issue in order to claim personal righteousness.

In contrast, God focused on the issue by asking about their disobedience: "Have you eaten from the tree whose fruit I commanded you not to eat?" (Genesis 3:11). He did not blame them but allowed them to own up to their sins. Now that we know that God is love, maybe he would have forgiven them if they had been honest with each other and with God, owned up to their sin, and asked for forgiveness. Instead, by standing firm on their side of the story, they incurred judgement that disfigured their relationships with God, each other, and all of creation.

We act similarly today. We are tempted to take advantage of one another, blame others to clear our name, or manipulate circumstances

> **(?)** Have you or someone you know been part of a conflict that turned out to be no more than blaming another individual rather than focusing on issues? How did that play out and what were the results?
>
> ....
> ....
> ....
> ....

for our selfish schemes. As the prophet Jeremiah later sums up in his observations of humans, "The human heart is the most deceitful of all things, and desperately wicked. Who really knows how bad it is?" (Jeremiah 17:9). Indeed, sometimes we blame the other because we ourselves lack clarity about the real issue or the honesty to own our role in the conflict. But we can also be honest and deal with others in righteousness. To do this well, we must intentionally focus on the real issues while rejecting the temptation to deceive or manipulate others for our selfish benefit.

Doing "all that you can to live in peace with everyone" means avoiding the blame-and-shame game that often characterizes relationships, especially in conflict. I have not met anyone working honestly to restore their relationship who is committed to blaming and shaming the other person. However, I have extensive experience of seeing people who, because they are committed to restoring their relationship, will go to any length to shoulder the blame, get the other person to work with them, and even make sacrifices in order to repair their relationship. They recognize that, to move forward, some of the blame must be absorbed to mend the relationship.

How to Clarify the Issue

You may have heard the sayings, "Keep the main thing the main thing" or "Major on the majors and not the minors." It is particularly tempting when in a conflict situation to be side-tracked by focusing on minor things and ignoring the real issues. Some people do this when they do not want to deal with the issue. Or perhaps they know they are wrong and are too stubborn or proud to acknowledge their situation. This can have untold consequences.

If you don't focus on the issue, you add more and more layers to the conflict until at some point you can't even remember what the original issue was. When we feel misunderstood and judged, we often want a chance to clear the air, state our original intentions, and explain what we did or meant.

The spiralling process can be stopped with the right attitude: a desire to understand the true causes, to understand each other, and collaborate to work things out. For this to work out well, each party must be willing to acknowledge their part in the conflict (what they did or did not do to cause it) and explore ways to mend the breach.

One principle I have learned for conducting mediation can be particularly beneficial in clarifying the real issue. I require the parties to prepare by writing down their side of the story in as much detail as possible. Writing gives people time to review their thoughts, distill the issues, and determine their real complaints. It can help to separate emotions from circumstances. I ask them to answer questions such as these:

1. Describe how this conflict started. When was the first time you noticed you were in disagreement? Include as many details as you remember.
2. What issues do you believe this conflict is about?
3. What has been your and the other person's role in the conflict?

Once I receive their responses, I ask permission to exchange the notes with the other party before our meeting. My discovery? Most people are surprised at the other person's understanding of the cause of the conflict. When their answers are honest, and they come prepared, they gain insight. They are also happy to set the record straight. This process helps them to hear each other and clarify the real issues they are fighting over. As they talk together with the goal of resolution, most gain a better understanding of the relationship and are able to move forward.

Writing and talking things over have a way of cutting through the clutter to highlight the core issues that might have led to the spiral. The questions have helped people to start imagining a possible solution so that when they come together, they can draft a set of agreed solutions or ways to properly deal with the issues. This process also helps reestablish trust, a key ingredient in transforming relationships.

For example, a while ago I met with two individuals sharing an apartment who were having issues with personal property. One person sought mediation, complaining that the other did not respect them and belittled them because of their ethnicity. This conflict had gone unresolved for a while, with each side piling on other issues.

After receiving the pre-mediation survey, I summarized what I saw as the issues the two parties were fighting over. The problems differed significantly from the verbal complaint filed in our offices before. The disrespect had nothing to do with ethnicity but had everything to do with lost trust due to one party using the other's supplies without permission. Since they did not talk about it, the assumptions grew, further entrenching the conflict.

I also remember how, in one of my first jobs, three social workers would go into the communities to meet with different community members and then file reports to their manager. We had some basic guidelines of where they needed to go regarding distance, how many people they needed to talk to within a period, and how many reports they needed to file to justify their positions. These numbers were established and reviewed often with the entire department's cooperation. We also ran with them for a few years and realized that what we required was feasible.

However, one social worker was not meeting the required number of visits and had fewer reports to bring back. The head of the social work department met with him several times and determined that he was either slow, not going out to the community in the way he claimed to be doing, or a combination of both. They feuded over this for several months with no solution.

I was the project manager, so when I heard of the brewing disagreement, I offered to meet with both the social worker and the head of the department. The social worker claimed that his female colleagues had an easier time talking to people in the community than it was for him as a man. As strange as this argument may sound, he firmly believed it and used it as his defence. He forgot that the head of the department, a man, had done this work for several years before and had met those quotas.

Clearly, he was offering a weak excuse rather than be accountable for his inability to perform his duties. We had to let him go because that attitude prevented him from being effective in his role.

Using the Pre-Mediation Questions

While the examples above describe how to use questions in preparation for working with a mediator, you don't necessarily need to involve a third party to find the pre-mediation questions helpful. Answering these questions can help to clarify the real issue in any conflict situation. If the other person is willing, you can each use these questions to write down your answers and swap them to kick-start a better, issue-focused conversation.

Even if the other person in the conflict is unwilling, you can still use these questions on your own. If you need to, let yourself vent your emotions in writing first. Get your emotions off your chest and calm down. Then take a more objective approach and answer the questions yourself. This can give you new insights.

Next, imagine what the other person might write as their answers. Suppose I am in a conflict with my sister. From what she said, how she acted, and what I know of her, does she seem to be focused on an issue different from the one I wrote down? Is there something in particular bothering her? What issue specifically provokes her strongest reaction? If I can do this with empathy, I might begin to see things from her perspective. When you do this, be sure to hold these ideas loosely to avoid making wrong assumptions.

When you meet with the other person, you can open the conversation by apologizing for the areas you have identified as your role in the conflict. You can also share what you thought the main issue was and ask whether your guesses at that person's perspective are relevant. Showing that you want to understand the other individual's perspective and are willing to take the first steps toward reconciliation can break down the barriers that blame has built.

You can also use these questions to help others in conflict by offering to be a mediator. Differences that involve positions of interest (i.e., what each party desires) often come with a level of emotional investment, making each person dig their heels in, insisting on their side of the story. So, if you were to talk with Remi on the side, he would probably convince you of his interpretation of the "facts." He most likely would leave out details of his inefficiency and lack of production and try to convince you that his manager hates him or wants him fired.

The Bible offers this as a warning, "The first to speak in court sounds right – until the cross-examination begins" (Proverbs 18:17).

This warning is beneficial when you counsel people in conflict. Don't be easily won over by any side of the story until you have had a chance to hear both sides and even to investigate a little more.

You will often discover that the issues central to the conflict differ greatly from when you trust only one side. For instance, if you were to talk to Muruku about Remi, he would show you the records for his production and state that he needs to meet the requirements. It may take deeper digging to clarify the real issue. Is he not able to perform at that level? Was he not trained to accomplish this amount of work? Are the production numbers set too high?

Suspending judgement when mediating is hard because we want to be on good terms with others, show love and support, or avoid being involved in other people's fights. Unfortunately, not exploring the details for both sides can lead us into a web of mistrust (and even conflict). Honesty among all the parties (including the mediator) is crucial to understanding a conflict and its eventual transformation.

Conclusion

In this chapter, we have seen how crucial it is to address the underlying causes of conflict and why we must avoid the temptation to focus on the other party as the problem. When we shift to addressing the issues, we can often positively resolve the issues and transform the relationship. Discovering, centring on, and clarifying the issue also helps us better understand the other party and engage each other honestly. The other person ceases to be the problem; the problem is the problem. Both sides embrace focusing on the problems rather than demonizing or making the other the enemy.

Remember our case study at the opening of the chapter? Let's revisit that story and see what might have caused the break and some possible ways to address the underlying issues.

Later that evening, Tati stopped by Remi's house. She was best friends with Remi's wife and was concerned about Remi and the family. In the conversation over dinner, Remi confided in her that Jelani wanted him fired. He felt blindsided. Jelani was Tati's manager, too, and a friend. Tati was confused. Tati tried to explain Jelani's attitude, but Remi was not convinced. He believed she hated him because he was from a different tribe.

A few days later, Tati returned to invite Remi and his wife and baby for dinner on the weekend. She also asked several other friends.

At Tati's home, Remi encountered Jelani. He could not believe it. What a setup! He wanted to escape, but it would be rude to leave when they had only just arrived. Plus, his wife was grateful to spend time with friends.

After dinner, Tati invited Jelani and Remi to the back porch. Tactfully, she brought up the situation in the office. She confided in them that, because she was friends with both of them, she felt it important to help them mend their relationship and save Remi's job.

Jelani went first. "I do not hate you, Remi. I am just going by the production numbers. Everyone in your position, including Tati, can produce beyond the set quotas. I am required to report these monthly. Muruku saw those and so he wanted to talk to you. He never talked to me at all."

"So, you did not report me to him?" Remi retorted.

"I swear, I never reported anything except filing the numbers."

"Look, I know you don't like me. People from your tribe do not like us anyway," Remi protested.

"My husband is from your tribe," Jelani asserted. "Why would you think I would hate all people like that? Why can't you believe that this is just about production? I am happy to help you meet your numbers if you want. Listen, all the other associates have a buddy system where we support one another. But you have chosen to work alone and not engage with others. So we all left you alone."

Remi felt ashamed at being exposed. He had nowhere to hide. "What do you mean you can help?"

"We are all family. But when you came in, you behaved differently because you had a national diploma and did not want to associate with others. We offered help, but you wouldn't take it. You also did not finish your training because you said you knew what to do. So, I do my job and report the numbers. Everyone else is working together. And guess what, no one has ever come short on numbers, only you." Jelani let the final statement hang as if to say, "You fool!"

"It is true, we do all work together, which means all the numbers are divided equally," Tati added.

"Why didn't anyone tell me?" Remi asked angrily.

"Remi, when you see a know-it-all fish, you let it fry itself in its own fat," Jelani chided. "If you are ready to jump out of the pan and join the rest in the pool, we are happy to have you," she concluded.

As is typical, Remi believed that his boss and others above him were singling him out. However, we now know that his attitude of non-cooperation and lack of proper training were likely the cause for his non-performance. In the conversations, we discover his assumptions were all wrong. A change would have to occur, one that addressed these areas of lack to allow Remi to work closely with his colleagues, who would support him in meeting his production quotas.

When people sit with each other and are interested in understanding and crafting a way forward, this can be an insightful process where each party discovers the real issues and their role. People gain a better experience of the relationship and can move forward. But that process must start with honesty about where each party stands and the real issues involved. It also means checking to see the "log in my eye" before I blame the other for the "speck in their eye". That is where we turn next in our journey toward conflict transformation.

Refer to the three pre-mediation questions listed earlier. Identify a conflict you are involved in, either currently or in the past. Try to answer the three questions as honestly as you can. If comfortable, approach the other party and ask them to do the same. Then, either with the help of a friend or just the two of you, meet up to talk through your notes. Document the results of your experience.

....

....

....

....

....

....

....

....

Group Discussion

1. Are there people in your community or society who have been overlooked, stereotyped, or mistreated because of their ethnicity or background? What are the origins of the opposing views about this people group, and what can be done to change that?
2. Pick an ongoing inter-community or societal conflict and try to tease the various issues from the perspectives of the parties involved.

I Have a Log in My Eye

Anansi was a respected community leader in a middle-class city suburb. He owned one of the houses with a corner lot, which was prime for an extension. His wife encouraged him to consider building "servants' quarter", a smaller rental unit, in order to earn income from their property. Anansi would be retiring in a few years, and this would be a way to earn some cash. His wife had also dealt with some illnesses and had not worked for several years.

However, Anansi was also the leader of the homeowners' association. Over the years, the association had tried to control unauthorized developments, and he had opposed any extensions to the original home plans in their neighbourhood. Once, when a member wanted to tear down their house and build a taller structure with several additional living units, Anansi protested. "If the neighbourhood becomes a high-density neighbourhood full of renters, the whole neighbourhood will change for the worse! You aren't content with what you have and couldn't care less about the rest of us!"

Of course, at that time, Anansi did not have the money to carry out his own developments. Now, his tune had changed. His son, Dee, a technology investor, offered to front the money for the development to assist his parents. Dee even got the plans for the redevelopment approved by an official in City Hall, as they attended the same school. He encouraged his parents to develop the property without delay.

As word got out that Anansi wanted to develop his lot, several neighbours were outraged. At a neighbourhood meeting, most members voted to stop all developments, citing community covenant rules. Many members were genuinely concerned that if they started granting permission for such developments, their neighbourhood would end up with many uncontrolled developments that would drive down the value of their properties. Other members were reacting because Anansi had vigorously opposed others from carrying out similar developments for many years. After the vote, the neighbours sent Anansi a letter detailing their opposition and threatening to sue him unless he stopped the development.

Dee consulted a lawyer friend, who told him that the community members had no standing under the law and their vote would not hold up in court. Dee thus urged his dad to proceed as soon as possible: "You are sitting on a gold mine that can secure your retirement!"

Anansi was not sure. He hated upsetting his neighbours this way, but he also needed the extra income. It wasn't as if he was building an apartment complex; it was just a small outbuilding. Surely that couldn't hurt anyone?

Logs and Specks

How often have you heard people in conflict say things like, "She does not value me at all!" or "I know he meant to hurt me in any way he could – he is evil!"? The other person is thus seen as not only unwilling to solve the problem at hand but is also uncooperative, deficient, or unreasonable. Many of us are guilty of making these exaggerations out of frustration. Even when we do not express it openly, our minds tell us that the other person has ill intentions and is out to get us.

At the same time, we underplay our role in the conflict and the breakdown of the relationship with excuses: "Everyone makes mistakes", "I had a bad day", or "I was not thinking well and didn't mean it." But we insist that the other person did not simply make a mistake like we did. They, of course, were intentional and calculating, determined to do harm.

We tend to paint ourselves and our motives as good while doubting or even painting the motives of others as suspect or even evil. This psychological bias has been extensively studied and is said to cause many broken relationships – interpersonal and otherwise.

Examine a recent conflict you had – or your friends had. What was your role in the conflict? Were you able to see your contributions to the break at the time or only after? Why or why not?

This rationale says, "They have a log in their eye; I only have a speck in mine." The log-and-speck metaphor comes from Jesus's famous teaching about not judging others and being honest about our brokenness and responsibility. He says:

> "Do not judge others, and you will not be judged. For you will be treated as you treat others. The standard you use in judging is the standard by which you will be judged. And why worry about a speck in your friend's eye when you have a log in your own? How can you think of saying to your friend, 'Let me help you get rid of that speck in your eye,' when you can't see past the log in your own eye? Hypocrite! First get rid of the log in your own eye; then you will see well enough to deal with the speck in your friend's eye" (Matthew 7:1-5).

Judgement here means seeing the other person as less than or worse than ourselves, or even evil, while exonerating ourselves. Once, when a group of religious leaders was getting ready to stone a woman accused of adultery, they asked Jesus's opinion on the case. Jesus said, "Let the one has never sinned throw the first stone." He pointed out that they judged her guilt to be worse than their own. Eventually, each person left, admitting to having their own areas of sin and guilt too (John 8:2-11).

Jesus warns against this tendency again using a story in Luke 18:9-14. He pits a man of God, a Pharisee, against a corrupt government official. The man of God comes to the place of worship and describes his goodness before God and people: "I am not like this corrupt official over there." He enumerates all the righteous things he does and the sinful things he avoids. The corrupt official knows he is a sinner, and humbly repents, saying, "God, be merciful to me, a sinner." Jesus concludes that this corrupt man should go home forgiven and at peace with God because he humbled himself.

Although primarily warning against pride, this story also applies to conflict transformation. Both men were in conflict with God due to their sins, but only one would admit it. The man who had an accurate view of himself resolved his dispute, whereas the person determined to look down on others did not. This connects with something similar that Paul teaches: "Don't be selfish; don't try to impress others. Be humble, thinking of others as better than yourselves" (Philippians 2:3). To do this well has to come from a proper assessment of self, as well as a recognition of the image of God and the value of others.

A Window on Our Blind Spots

"The log in your eye" is a blind spot. You cannot see it, but others are aware of it. A psychological review theory called the Johari Window visually depicts how we all have areas of our lives known to us and other areas hidden from our awareness. Developed in 1955 by two research psychologists, Joseph Luft and Harrington Ingham (hence Jo-Hari), it has been used as a model for mapping personality awareness. This tool can help you acknowledge that your perspective of yourself may be distorted and incomplete, thus helping you stay humble and objective during any conflict. It also encourages us to expand our self-awareness.

The Johari Window is divided into four quadrants. Quadrant one includes the things we *know* about ourselves and can speak about. This area is also *open* or *known* to those around us, so it is shared information. Quadrant two contains things about us that are *blind* or *unknown* to us but *known* to others. These are things that people can point out about us because they have observed us or our relationship.

	Known to self	Unknown to self
Known to others	**Open self** Information about you that both you and others know.	**Blind self** Information about you that you don't know but others do know.
Unknown	**Hidden self** Information about you that you know but others don't know.	**Unknown self** Information about you that neither you nor others know.

In most cases, a close friend or family member can help highlight areas in quadrant two, i.e., areas that are *blind* to us. Asking them whether they notice anything about you that you might not be aware of can be an excellent exercise to engage in as part of your growth. If you do, take time to consider what you discover. Did you uncover anything new that surprised you? Can you see any patterns for how the highlighted areas have influenced your relationships with others?

Quadrant three is for all the areas of our lives that are *known* to us but *hidden* from others. These are our personal "secrets." No one will know these secrets unless we tell them. The last quadrant contains all the things *unknown* to both us and others. Think about when someone does something and they (and those around them) say, "That was a total surprise. I never thought I was capable of such a thing." They might be operating from that *unknown* space.

Note – the quadrants are not always equal. As we grow in genuine self-understanding and self-discovery, the areas of knowledge about ourselves expand, and the *hidden* and *unknown* areas of our lives shrink.

Explore who you are using the Johari Window below. Fill out the left column with areas you know about yourself, including what others have talked to you about.

Known to me and others:	Known only to others:
Known only to me:	**Unknown**

Professionals counselling people in conflict often encourage the parties to entertain the possibility that there are areas of their lives they might not know very well. It might be that the other party can see these, and so be able to help better address the issues.

I am a strong advocate of self-assessment. But I advocate even more for allowing others to evaluate us if we genuinely seek to learn more about ourselves.

I Might Not Be as Innocent as I Think

When we find ourselves in a conflict, we must consider ways we might be guilty of contributing to the conflict too. Sometimes, honest introspection can reveal that we are not always as innocent as we may be tempted to think. There are many tools for introspection that can help you in that process. For example, the Jesuit tradition follows a process called the examen: an honest, reflective review of oneself in the presence of God. It can also be used to review an issue or a day. It uses simple questions such as: "How was I present today or at an event?" or "How did I feel or see God in my life today?" One can build on these questions to thoroughly examine both self and reality. It also exposes areas of concern and may help you focus on the need for prayer and action.

This type of introspection is possible for an individual as well as a team. One of the results of this process of personal review may be discovering areas you do not know enough about or even areas where your views may need to be corrected, or vice versa.

While what I recommend may not technically be an examen spiritual practice, here are a few questions to help with honest introspection specifically tailored to a conflict situation.

How does my action or inaction contribute to the conflict?

What did I do (or not do) that led us to this place? This is the most crucial question in the introspection process. It entails an honest assessment of your responsibility towards the other person and for the circumstances that led to the situation. The aim is not simply to find a culprit to blame for the conflict as a whole, but to evaluate the specific words uttered, the actions taken, the inactions, and the damage caused. It outlines anything that could be considered your contribution for actively or inactively feeding into the breakdown of relations.

How do my values or expectations contribute to the conflict?

Our expectations or desires for how we want things to happen can cause conflict. The expectations we have of others can cause conflict. And then there are expectations around the other person's ability to bear with us: "They should understand my perspectives and any weaknesses I have. Failure to understand means they have a problem – it's not my fault."

My counsellor friend also highlighted how, in her practice, she challenges the parties to assume the other person's role and try to imagine which of their expectations are realistic and untenable. It challenges the parties to consider their biases and their positions in reacting to the other individual. She has also learned to encourage parties to lay out their expectations of the other going forward and to voice these in the presence of their partner so that they can discuss them and agree on what is feasible.

How does my attitude or approach to conflict contribute to the conflict?

As discussed elsewhere, we all have innate styles for how we relate to conflicts, ranging from avoidance to addressing the conflicts head-on. It is helpful to ask: How do I tend to react to a conflict situation? How does that help resolve the problem or escalate the tensions? Sometimes, our attitudes or positions are the problem.

In an NGO I worked for in the past, I had a new boss whose leadership style was very different from what I was used to. In our first meeting, I felt he was questioning my competence on a project I was running. I reacted and stonewalled him, refusing to give him more information. I felt that he had no right to challenge me on something I had done for many years and with documented success. As a result, we immediately found ourselves locked into a conflict that lasted for several months.

In my effort to "preserve myself," I rejected his input, which may have allowed me to learn more and maybe even improve the project. It was not until the project was withdrawn from me that I saw my foolishness. By then, it was too late. I had been bitter and unhelpful. As I reflected on how I had reacted, I could see how I had caused the breach and that it did not have to turn out this way. I had been too proud, unnecessarily uncompromising, and short-sighted. The leadership was thus right to pull me off the project because I was not the best person to run it, especially in how I was going about it without outside input.

These three questions can significantly help to centre your thoughts around your own responsibility and contribution to the conflict without casting blame. You may come up with further questions that would better guide this process, as long as they don't lead you back to blaming and assigning all the responsibility to the other party.

Of course, remaining unbiased and objective in times of conflict is difficult. However, we can pursue honest introspection and be humble about our brokenness. Remember, identifying our responsibility is part of the diagnosis that can help find workable solutions to transform the battle and save the relationship, which is our goal.

Perhaps, after the review, you can honestly say, "I have no role in this conflict. The other party is the only cause." If so, you are still on the right track to removing the log from your eye and finding proper processes for addressing the issues.

A Pastor's Blind Spots

Getting to know ourselves better can foster lasting conflict transformation – but we often need others to help us understand ourselves! The goal for growing any relationship is to develop the *shared* areas with others and explore, with their help, the *blind* spots of our lives. Our blind spots and unknown areas often mean we do not acknowledge our responsibility in conflicts, because we do not understand ourselves as much as we imagine.

Conflict is an excellent way to expand your self-awareness. Often, other people point out our blind spots – and not always in the kindest terms! If we are wise and open to learning, we may take the opportunity to expand our self-knowledge. Too often, we ignore their warnings to our own peril.

I witnessed this firsthand after college when I moved to Nairobi to find a job. I got involved in a church, leading the youth ministry and serving as an intercessor.

One Sunday morning, the pastor announced that he was leaving and had decided to break ties with the denomination and start his own congregation under a new name. He accused the national denominational leaders and the local elders' board of trying to "quench the spirit" and hold him back from serving with his complete set of gifts. He equated this situation with Paul and Barnabas parting company over Mark. He was Barnabas, he said, wanting more from the relationship, and the elders could not deliver this. He invited all "led by the Spirit" to move on with him to set up the new church. Meetings were to start the following week at a location he was renting.

We were confused. There had been no details about the goings-on or the sudden change. I was unhappy with how the pastor blamed everyone else but himself. Plus, this felt uncomfortably rushed. There were too many unanswered questions: What issues occasioned the break, and what attempts were made to heal this relationship? Why did the Board of Elders not issue a statement or provide further information? We heard rumours, spread mainly by one of the elders that the pastor wanted to control and run the church as a personal outfit, which was against the denominational setup. That was hard to believe because the pastor seemed humble and agreeable, someone who did not enjoy being in the limelight.

More than 75 per cent of the congregation followed him to the new location, even with all these questions. I did too. We liked the pastor and wanted to continue enjoying his leadership and teachings. He explained his side of the story. He had been in an ongoing tussle with the denomination leadership for more than four years. He wanted permission to move the congregation in a different direction, including allowing women to preach, using more contemporary worship music, and participating in ecumenical projects with other churches. The elders and denominational leaders would not allow any of these and threatened to fire him if he continued to make such demands. The pastor had no choice but to move on. Now was the time.

Many of us believed him. We went on to support the church in the newly rented space, and the congregation grew as he allowed greater expressions of faith and outreach. The new freestyle worship services attracted more younger people in town too. Slowly, the pastor was vindicated for having left the more traditional structures behind. His wife was ordained as a fellow pastor and they hired worship and youth pastors as well. Everything was looking up.

Unfortunately, less than three years on, everything around the church imploded. The pastor now controlled every aspect of the ministry, though he had appointed a few elders. One of them tipped off government officials about financial mismanagement by the pastor. The government ordered an audit of the church books, and it was found that the pastor and his wife were indeed siphoning off church resources for personal use. They also uncovered that the pastor had influenced political leaders to allocate a public piece of land to the church building but registered it as his personal property. Most of us left the church.

We realized that the pastor had character flaws that needed to be addressed, some of which the previous elders' board had tried to hold him accountable for. Instead of submitting to their discipline, he chose to pursue his own goals, separate from any accountability. He was not as innocent as he had claimed to be, after all!

This is not new or unusual. I have seen other situations where people are not ready to submit to an accountability process that would help them learn something they really need. I once had a co-worker whose annual evaluations urged him to prioritize his work and fulfil assignments more punctually. Instead, he left the NGO in a huff, arguing that people did not like him. When I met him two years later, he had been cut from the other organization he had gone to work for. They had pointed out the same issues he had run away from where we worked together. He wished he had learned at the first NGO, where the environment supported that. He regretted that, at this point, he had to learn the hard way by being unemployed.

The Bible strongly encourages accountability. Paul, writing to the Corinthians, encourages believers to take their fellowships seriously. Instead of taking cases to non-Christian courts, believers should be able to hold each other accountable, especially those who are sinning (1 Corinthians 5:12). In Hebrews, the author urges the believers to stay in fellowship, to "not neglect our meeting together, as some people do, but encourage one another, especially now that the day of his return is drawing near" (Hebrews 10:25). The reasons for this are not just encouragement, but also to be a corrective force for each other. How else do you know you are on the right track? It is only by having relations with others that are close enough that they can encourage you when in need but also can tell you when you are wrong.

That accountability also stretches beyond responsibility to a community to the final judgement. All humans will be held accountable to the ultimate authority, God, at the end of time. Jesus teaches that this will separate sheep and goats, the good and the evil (Matthew 25:31-46). Paul sums it as a time to account for our lives: "We will each receive whatever we deserve for the good or evil we have done in this earthly body" (2 Corinthians 5:10).

They Might Not Be as Guilty as I Think

When we feel hurt, we risk assigning blame to the other person. We are sure the other is responsible and rush in to condemn their actions and motives.

Practising seeing the log in my eye first means suspending judgement long enough to learn the true intentions of the other. This is especially important when confronted with a situation where an individual's character and history may be inconsistent with the current situation. In most cases, the other is not the monster I was tempted to think they had become. They turned out not to be as guilty as I thought. To get there, I must be patient, hold off on assigning blame, and be curious to learn the circumstances of their actions (or inaction).

A lawyer and his brother crossed swords over a strange misunderstanding. Like most siblings, they were good friends but still had minor disagreements. The lawyer was offered a partnership at a law firm where he worked, but this required an investment of a sum he did not have. The controlling partners needed an answer within the week. This was an opportunity of a lifetime, and he could not pass it up.

The lawyer called his dad and requested to use the family farm as collateral to borrow the money and invest in the partnership. He promised to repay the loan as soon as possible. The dad agreed. The lawyer drove up to their home village, picked up the title deed to the property, and used it to borrow the money needed to invest in the law firm.

As the family celebrated the lawyer's acceptance as a partner at the law firm, the information about using the family farm as collateral came up. The brother asked why he had not been consulted over the decision. To him, this seemed like a conspiracy to deny him his rightful inheritance! The family, he felt, had treated him with less respect than his lawyer brother because he was not as successful. Or was it because he was the second born and had been closer to his mother than to his dad growing up?

The lawyer and his parents felt ashamed for leaving the brother out of this crucial decision. The lawyer had not thought to call him since he knew his brother would not have the cash. But they had still gone ahead without notifying him. It was not until they explained the urgency and apologized for handling the situation so carelessly that the brother calmed down. Although he had initially assumed that they had evil motives, when he learned the details he understood their reasons for acting as they did. It had been an emergency that needed to be handled as quickly as possible. But they all agreed that, for future actions like these, no rushed decisions would be made without proper consultation to be sure everyone was on board.

Intentions and motives may only be partially known to the person carrying out the act. We say "partially known" because, in some cases, there might not be a clear motive for an action (or inaction). It might be no more than a random happening, a mistake. This is more reason to wait to properly understand before assigning blame. Discovering all that might have gone on is not always easy. Determining just how much responsibility the other party carries requires patience, tolerance, and a lot of grace.

The person may not be aware of their responsibility and may need to go through a similar process of cleaning out their eyes to be sure they can clearly see their role in the situation. And they may not be ready to be as honest with themselves as you are. In that case, you are forced to wait, even give them space.

> **?**
>
> **Are there times when you assumed someone was wrong only to find out later that they weren't? How did you react before and after?**
>
> ....
>
> ....
>
> ....
>
> ....

During the Covid-19 pandemic, at the university where I teach, the administration decided overnight to change all courses to online learning. This was agreed at a high-level university administrators' meeting, and an email was then sent to faculty and students informing them of the change. As expected, many faculty members were frustrated that the administration had not asked for their input. They just issued instructions to change the teaching format without warning or time for preparation.

As a result, the faculty forum leaders fired back a letter accusing the leadership of heavy-handedness. A quick video meeting was called where the administration offered more information that had not been provided to the faculty previously. They first apologized for the rushed decision but also explained that several students had contracted the virus. By state law, they were required to act to contain the spread. Out of caution, they decided that their best option was to stop those students' classes from meeting, and to do that decided to shut the whole university down. The final decision of the meeting between the faculty and the administration was still to shut down the campus, but with a promise to try to work through a process for gathering input before making drastic decisions that affected the entire university community. As it turned out, the faculty had been too quick to make conclusions about the administration's motives and approach.

Why We Focus on the Negative

Why are we so quick to suspect other people's motives? It may be because we remember negative memories more readily than positive ones.

Remembering pain is a natural survival instinct to protect us from further injuries. A young child remembers to stop sticking their fingers into the fire after the first time. When she sees the fire again, she remembers the pain. This saves her from continual hurt. We can do the same thing to protect ourselves from emotional injury, especially if there is a history of wounds.

Unfortunately, storing the details of these situations can hinder our relationships with others. The negative assumptions colour our views about the other so that anything else they do, good or bad, is only seen through this experience. We begin to shout "Fire!" at anything.

When we remember moments of relational hurt at times of conflict, we may sometimes miss the value of wholesome relations that could benefit us. In trying to avoid further pain, we are tempted to forget to consider the circumstances. However, the circumstances are not always similar enough to mean we will be hurt in the same way. For instance, in my primary-school days, one neighbour used to bully me. Although he and I have gone on to be successful in similar ways, I have sadly not cared to seek any relations with him, even though I believe that would benefit both of us.

Fortunately, because we already know that negative interactions make a more significant impression, we can balance those with more positive interactions. Researchers Drs John Gottman and Robert Levenson, having studied couples in conflict for 15 minutes, could predict with 90 per cent accuracy which couples would still be together 10 years later. In the happy couples, there were at least five positive interactions during conflict for each negative interaction. Including positive interactions in your relationship – and even in your conflict conversations – can increase trust and build the relationship.

Conclusion

In the case study of Anansi above, he was quick to assume the ill motives of his neighbours when they wanted to develop their plots. But when he found himself in the same situation, he was much more understanding of the complexities. Perhaps it had not been greed but business sense or family needs motivating his neighbours. While he had seen only disregard for the community in their proposals, he now realized that the same choice could be made from a place of care for one's sickly wife.

How would he look into the mirror of his intentions and past actions to act consistently with what the community agreed upon? Did having the opportunity to benefit himself excuse him from his responsibility to the rest of the community, even if the law did not restrict him? This is a temptation we face as we deal with others. We need to look beyond the law to "love others as we love ourselves."

Anansi could refuse to reflect on his actions and intentions. He could plough forward with the development, angering his neighbours, and maybe find himself dealing with an expensive court case. Relationships might be broken and living in the community might become difficult.

True honesty would entail being honest with his neighbours by sharing his plans. He may need to look at how he hurt others through his heavy-handed stance on non-development. He could apologize to all those he insulted in the past. Instead of going forward with the project without the community's approval, he may want to humbly appeal to them to seek a different process to rectify restrictions that benefit the majority.

After a comprehensive review of his circumstances and what he would be putting the family and community through, Anansi decided that a more honest direction would be to halt the development plans. He did not want to be the pariah of the community by pursuing a selfish goal, even though that would benefit him and his family.

He worked with a financial advisor, who helped him explore other alternatives to fund his retirement. For one, he had another property in the village to which he and his wife could relocate. Life in the village was cheaper and slower, which they would appreciate once they had retired. He could then rent out his house in the city, giving him a significant amount to live on. The community would not need to sue him and they could keep their friendships intact. It was a win-win for all!

Learning more about ourselves prepares and teaches us how to handle conflict with others. This learning can begin with personally evaluating our personality, upbringing, and influences. To take the logs out of our eyes, we must be in community with others who can point out our blind spots and help us grow. Of course, just learning about oneself does not automatically lead to growth. It takes humility to apply these lessons and to want to change. In the following chapter, we explore this idea of change further because we will only be able to transform our conflicts if we are open to change, especially changing our minds.

(?)

Thinking of a conflict that you were recently involved in, reflect on the following questions:

1. How did my action or inaction contribute to the conflict?

. . . .

. . . .

. . . .

2. How did my values or expectations contribute to the conflict?

. . . .

. . . .

. . . .

3. How did my attitude or approach to conflict contribute to the conflict?

. . . .

. . . .

. . . .

Group Discussion

1. Why is it so difficult to have a true view of ourselves?
2. Share with the group from your Johari window on page 132. Ask the group members how they see you. Use it to fill in the top right box. Is this how you see yourself? Why or why not?

8

A Mind Change Is Good

The pastor of Calvary Community Church (CCC) began a sermon series on politics and citizenship in preparation for the upcoming national election. He urged his congregation to seek God's wisdom and carefully research what the candidates stood for and how they would govern. He said that Christians owe it to themselves to be educated about issues and engage all sides without judging or condemning. "We don't have to vote similarly," he said, "but we have a responsibility to be open to new and different ideas before deciding."

The CCC Southside home group met on a Tuesday night in Kirwa's sitting room to discuss the pastor's sermon series. Milka, a schoolteacher, said, "I'm so glad we finally have a Christian candidate! But I can't understand why Pastor Kioni hasn't invited

Mr Mulongo or his representatives to church or discussed how we all need to vote to support him."

Mr Ngoni, a businessman, jumped in. "What makes you so sure that Pastor Kioni even supports him?"

"Of course he supports him. Church leaders all over the country support him. It's plain to see that God is appointing him for such a time as this when our family values need a defender. But our pastor doesn't seem to see the urgency. We really need to be mobilizing the church. If we don't come out in numbers, there is no telling what might happen to this country."

Mr Ngoni replied, "Have you been paying attention to the reports? Everyone knows that, as finance minister, Mr Mulongo defrauded the country. I don't care if he calls himself Christian. He's only using the label to garner votes, and I won't fall for it."

"Those accusations are baseless. There's no evidence. That's why even the court couldn't prosecute him. It's all a setup by that pesky opposition leader. Don't tell me you're voting for him!"

"Why not? At least he promises transparency laws, which means that everyone will declare where they got their wealth. I'd much rather have someone honest than a hypocrite who takes the Christian name only to ruin the reputation of Christianity."

"So, you would rather ruin our country? Your candidate plans to indoctrinate all our children with his new curriculum. We need to take a stand for morality and protect vulnerable young minds! It's people like you who don't take the name of Christian seriously!"

"At least I'm not a blind sheep like you!"

A Learning Attitude

To maintain and grow our relationships, we must learn, especially from conflict. Learning new information might lead us to change our mind when needed. This willingness takes a level of maturity and a lot of humility. However, the benefits are enormous. A conflict can be addressed much more quickly, and more positive solutions can be found. When we are open to new information, we learn, improve, and become more understanding and aware.

Seeing the positive results this produces in situations we are working through will likely encourage our desire to have similar learning attitudes in the future. Our success will set us up for more transformation of future conflicts. Maybe you are not yet convinced. Hopefully, by the end of this chapter, you will have changed your mind!

Wisdom, Not Weakness

Many people see a change of mind as a weakness and look down on people who do so. This often happens when power plays a significant role in entrenching fear and unnecessary subordination. Some cultures regard confrontation as shameful; people do not want to be seen as controversial or breaking communal harmony. Therefore, people are forced to bear unnecessary pain even where they could easily address the issues with others. Others, especially those with higher status, try to "save face" by sticking to their views and positions. This can cause many unresolved conflicts to fester.

In some communities, especially patriarchal societies, men are socialized to believe "they know" or need to look like they know because that is what it means to "be a man". Unfortunately, when men don't know something, they may make up information or be rigid about their positions. That is seen to be better than the shame of acknowledging that they had to learn from someone they consider to be of lower status. You can see how this causes problems. But if your culture tells you that this is how you need to behave to look like you are in control, then the temptation is real, and it takes some re-learning to approach these situations differently.

A change of mind does not necessarily mean that you are frivolous or do not have a proper grasp of the situation. You may be well informed and even correct in your argument. Still, you come to the conversation thinking that if the other party has information to help you learn something new, you will happily change your position. You will engage in open communication to help determine the truth about an issue in order to move forward more positively.

Changing our minds signals maturity and wisdom, not a lack of knowledge or weakness. Indeed, despite the cultural values we mention above, cultures all over the world have proverbs and sayings about the wisdom of changing your mind:

- "True power comes through cooperation and silence." – Ghanaian
- "To agree to have dialogue is the beginning of a peaceful resolution." – Somali
- "Patience is the key that solves all problems." – Sudanese
- "The wise listen to her mind, the foolish to the mob." – Chinese
- "A wise man changes his mind, a fool never will." – Spanish
- "When the music changes, then the rhythm of the dance must change also." – Tuareg

The writer of Proverbs, a very practical book of the Bible on wise living, often encourages acting on new information and changing our minds where needed. In some cases, it warns that by not doing so we would be acting foolishly:

- "A prudent person foresees danger and takes precautions. The simpleton goes blindly on and suffers the consequences" (Proverbs 22:3).
- "Let the wise listen to these proverbs and become even wiser. Let those with understanding receive guidance" (Proverbs 1:5).
- "A truly wise person uses few words; a person with understanding is even-tempered" (Proverbs 17:27).

- "The first to speak in court sounds right – until the cross-examination begins" (Proverbs 18:17).

The fact that most cultures and the Bible speak with such force about changing our minds should challenge us to take it seriously. It means that unwillingness to change our minds when needed is foolish, irrespective of what we have come to believe.

Being willing to change our minds is often the first step toward resolving conflict not only with others, but also with God. Consider the relationship between Jesus and the Jewish religious leaders. Many in Israel at the time of Jesus expected a kingly Messiah, a political leader who would deliver them from the Roman occupation. This person would rule in place of King David.

But Jesus came as a Messiah calling people to repent and return to God, which was more in line with the role of a prophet than a kingly position. Jesus did not meet their expectations. What's more, in calling them to repent, he urged them to change their minds and their direction in life.

Some of the religious leaders were indeed willing to change their minds. Nicodemus sought new information from Jesus to help him understand Jesus better. Joseph of Arimathea believed in Jesus. But most people refused. When Jesus was taken to court, they could find no evidence to condemn him, but they were already committed to putting him to death. The people killed him because they were unwilling to change their hearts and minds.

At an NGO I worked for, I saw a remarkable example of a willingness to change one's mind and repent. The accountant prepared a report for the finance director to present at the board meeting. The finance director was unhappy with the accountant's conclusions about the NGO's overall financial position. Since the accountant was younger and less experienced, the finance director tried to make the accountant change the report to lie about the findings.

However, the young accountant knew that to do this would be unethical and might even cost him his career when the auditors came around. He thus declined, despite the pressure. Instead, he offered to discuss the report thoroughly with the director to find ways to present the same information to the board without raising unnecessary alarms. He also offered to help correct the accounting processes going forward so the organization could comply for the upcoming years.

To stand up against an influential director was a bold and potentially career-ending move, and we all feared he would be fired. However, he stood on principle, not attacking the director directly, and humbly offered to focus on correcting the problems.

Because of the accountant's humble approach, he won over the director. The director not only invited the accountant to the board meeting to present the report together, which was unheard of, but also owned up to the mistakes. He also presented the plan to correct the mistakes: the accountant would oversee those corrections and return to the board the following year with a better report. The plan was well received, and a crisis was averted. This was possible because the finance director was willing to listen and learn from his junior in a rare way for leaders at the time.

Escaping the Expectation Black Holes

An area we frequently need to change our minds about is our desires and expectations. Expectations are a powerful driver of our relationships. We all come to relationships, especially long-term ones, with many expectations. This is normal. In fact, our ability to think about the future and have hope are special characteristics that distinguish us from animals and help us carry on in life. If our expectations are low, we may be delighted when the individuals we encounter exceed them. But when the other person or the relationship does not live up to our hopes, we can feel disappointed and hurt. Often, our expectations are unrealistic or misplaced.

Black holes in the universe have such a strong pull of gravity that anything that comes near is sucked in, and even light cannot escape. Like a dangerous black hole, unrealistic expectations can swallow up relationships. When unrealistic expectations are not met, it is easy for us to find an excuse not to keep trying to save the relationship during a conflict.

Another type of unrealistic expectation in our relationships is what I call score-keeping. Score-keeping is the argument that the other person's efforts should always match your actions in a relationship. With this belief, people tend to keep track of their good deeds and the offences of others. If they ever give more than the other person to the relationship, they inform the other person an equal contribution is owed or overdue.

Let me illustrate this further. Two friends disagree over who should pay for a meal. One of them argues that because they paid the last time, the other should step up and pay. Or someone highlights that they cleaned a shared space, and the other needs to step in and do more. Although these are reasonable expectations, they must be negotiated and not be blanket expectations. Otherwise, the relationship becomes dependent on who did the most. While mutual giving is essential to a relationship, enforcing it as a transactional duty sucks all the love or goodwill out of the actions. Instead of being motivated by love, people are motivated by obligation or guilt, which doesn't build up the relationship.

A counsellor colleague once told me about a couple who, years into their relationship, had a growing number of conflicts among them. They determined to explore what might be the cause and sought help from a marriage counsellor. She helped them dig up the realities of their expectations for the other. The wife expected her husband to be the ultimate lover and provider – like Superman. The husband expected the wife to be kind, loving, and submissive to his authority. As they worked through their expectations, the counsellor helped them establish more realistic expectations that were achievable and agreed upon.

Until then, this couple had been engaged in an exciting Hollywood-type fantasy of marriage. Like unrealistic expectations, fantasy imagines perfection, where no one hurts or faces difficulties. As the rest of this book has emphasized, relationships are complex and offer opportunities to experience brokenness and injury. Getting into a relationship with someone and expecting it to be all roses is a fantasy. And when you hold on to this dream, you tend not to work for change when you face problems or conflict. Instead, when the fantasy fails – which, in most cases, it will – the frustration may lead you to walk away in disappointment and pain.

Of course, differing expectations in relationships are inevitable. This is partly because relationships are constantly changing. A conflict can accelerate this change. What do we do when that happens and shifts what we can reasonably expect from a relationship? We can either sign up for disappointment and blame others and ourselves or revise our expectations and seek a way forward. Viewed this way, conflicts clarify expectations and dispel some of our perceptions of others.

What is an expectation you held that impacted one of your relationships?

. . . .

. . . .

. . . .

. . . .

Adjusting expectations is a learning process that requires a willingness to change your mind. The only way to clarify expectations is through experience and discussing it with the other person. You can talk through expectations either before engaging in a deeper relationship or as you go through experiences that challenge each other's expectations.

My marriage counsellor friend uses a technique to help couples re-evaluate their expectations, which you might find helpful. She has each person (whether in conflict or not) draw three columns. In one column, they list their expectations of the other person. In the other column, they write where that expectation came from such as from their family of origin, past relationship, or learned belief. The third column evaluates how the other person or the relationship meets those expectations.

The two individuals then exchange notes. The counsellor then asks the couple to discuss the areas that surprised them. She then guides them in developing shared hopes and expectations that are clear to both parties and which they commit to accomplishing.

My friend says there are always surprises even among the most loving and committed couples. Voicing their privately held hopes and expectations helps the couples overcome potential traps in unrealized dreams. The best results come from open-minded couples who learn from each other and then change their expectations and relationship based on this new or re-learned information.

When you discuss your expectations with the other person, evaluate your expectations, especially in light of new information or better knowledge. See where you – or both of you – could make changes or accept some things as they are. For example, if you discover that someone else cannot truly meet a need as you expected, it is best to change it on your end. Holding on to an unrealistic expectation will frustrate you and drag the relationship down. Remember, you can only change yourself, not the other person.

Conflicts around expectations are not a problem only in marriage. One of my friends joined the company where her cousin was a senior partner and owner. She was excited about hanging out with her successful cousin, who was several years older and someone she looked up to. The cousin had helped her get the job, so she expected that her cousin would be cordial, mentor her, and even support her progress in the company.

The older cousin had other ideas, however. She did not want this to be seen as a nepotistic relationship, having given her cousin the job as a special favour. As a result, she kept her professional distance, acting business-like whenever they were together in the office.

The younger cousin could not understand why her older cousin was warm and engaging at family meetings, but in the office she acted as if she did not know her, or worse, as if she was like all other employees. It wasn't until the two cousins sat down to clear the air that they both realized their differing expectations were negatively affecting their relationship.

The Dividing Lines

Sometimes we need to change our minds not simply about an issue or expectation but our attitude toward a group of people. Like much of this book, I focus primarily on interpersonal relations, but division grows from person to person to affect an entire community.

In most societies today, rigid lines divide people. Politics, religious beliefs, ethnicities, racial differences, class, and more are important aspects of people's identities and communities. Unfortunately, because people have such strong bonds with other people who hold the same identities, they can also define themselves against those outside of that group. The resulting "us versus them" dichotomies can escalate to division and enmity.

Crafty leaders, like politicians, know how to manipulate these divisions for their selfish gains. In Africa, for instance, politicians commonly whip up tribal affiliations, regional backgrounds, and sometimes even religious differences, claiming they will be better leaders. Instead of governing with the good of the whole country in mind, they see themselves as representing "their people" who have their same identity. Cases of ethnic atrocities mixed up with politics and religion are all too familiar on the continent, with results like the 1994 Rwanda genocide, Kenya's 2007 post-election violence, and ongoing regional conflicts in Nigeria.

This phenomenon of aligning with particular identities is not unique to Africa. Many other societies also split into separate identities whenever it suits them. For example, in the 1990s, parts of Eastern Europe (Serbia, Croatia, and Macedonia) divided up along ethnic lines – some even resulting in war – and new countries were formed according to ethnicity. In parts of Asia, like Cambodia and Vietnam, ethnicity, religion, and politics have been used to formulate philosophies about governance and the unworthiness of other groups, leading to millions of people being sacrificed at these ideological altars. This rise in nationalistic attachments has been growing worldwide in recent years, with more groups leaning towards people who are just like them and openly despising or intentionally excluding others. Even within historically open democracies like the US and Europe, protectionist right-wing sentiments and associated groups have grown exponentially in the last few years. This has caused untold levels of conflict and even wars.

In hindsight, these atrocities might appear to be uninformed and unfortunate, but they are all driven by certainty in our convictions. No matter where you are from, we are all socialized into a particular ethnic, racial, class, or religious group. Unfortunately, that upbringing also makes it easy to believe that our communities are better than others.

Humans can either hold on to certain learned beliefs, like thinking our group is the best, or we can learn about and accept others. One key component to preventing differences from escalating into conflict is being open to re-examining our beliefs about the other group.

An excellent biblical example is Peter in the New Testament (Acts 10) and his relationship with the Gentiles (non-Jews). Peter, like all other Jews, was brought up to regard all Gentiles with a certain level of contempt. But, after Jesus had been resurrected and ascended to heaven, the Holy Spirit gave Peter a vision. In the vision, the Spirit commanded Peter to eat food commonly eaten by Gentiles, which would have been against Jewish culinary laws. In doing so, the Holy Spirit revealed that Peter should not despise others or judge them by their ethnicity and race. It's not just the Jews who were God's people – anyone was welcome.

This new information helped Peter change his mind. When the servant to a Gentile master showed up at the door, Peter accompanied him in obedience to the vision and went on to relate with them as instructed by God.

We know that Peter did not fully break away from his tradition, even with this dramatic event. Peter later backslid into his Jewish upbringing and forgot the vision to accept all people as equals. He did not interact freely with Gentiles. Paul later confronted him about this hypocrisy (Galatians 2).

As Christians, it is often a challenge to relate to all people as people who bear the image of God without considering ourselves as better than they are. Indeed, Paul admonishes: "Don't be selfish; don't try to impress others. Be humble, thinking of others as better than yourselves" (Philippians 2:3).

Facing the Facts

But how do you change your mind without being carried away by every point of view and piece of information? This is becoming increasingly difficult in a world where everyone believes they are right or is encouraged to think they are. Social media is partially to blame. The ease of posting unproven information and opinions as truth to the world has eroded our trust in facts. It is good to be discerning, but taking a sceptical approach to everything leads to doubting even the most factual information. Or we weigh it equally with our opinions and hunches and then discard new information if it doesn't align. We are confused and rarely convinced, even when we do need to change our minds.

In relationships, facts and truth matter. Of course, they are not the only things that matter in relationships, but without facts conversation will quickly stall in "my opinions against whoever else I am relating to." Sometimes I am wrong, and hearing the information from someone else should help me reconsider or even denounce my position.

As we said before, we all come to relationships with perceptions and perspectives, some of which could well be wrong or uninformed. Sometimes we come to an issue believing we have the best information – until we hear the other side and it becomes clear that we have been way off base. Occasionally, we must be open-minded to changing our stance if our relationships are to thrive. Otherwise, we might face unnecessary conflict and harm our relationships.

Seeking the truth involves being willing to interrogate information gaps to find out what we know and do not know about the circumstances. Our interpretation of information may be biased, wrong, or even based on past experiences. These can obscure objectivity. To avoid that, we need to honestly account for our and others' assumptions, misinterpretations, and perceptions to help arrive at an informed position. This is neither an easy, nor short process. We are often tempted to rush to judgement, casting others as malicious and ourselves as saints. But we need to take this time if we are to navigate conflicts and develop our relationships.

Delay Judgement

Since it is often harder to change our position after we have strongly argued for it, one technique that can make it easier to change your mind is to delay making a judgement. Delaying judgement here means stepping back, evaluating the circumstances, and coming to an informed decision on your position. It also means asking ourselves whether we have any assumptions or stereotypes that could cause us to jump to conclusions.

We all have a limited view of most circumstances we find ourselves in. Until we have had the opportunity to think through and listen to others, it is difficult to completely understand an issue, especially when the issue is as emotional as conflicts can be. Most issues we face when relating to others require a few minutes or hours to evaluate. This will help you protect and grow your relationships.

We are prone to react immediately to circumstances, often without having the complete picture. I sometimes respond too rashly when someone acts in a way I did not expect. Before I learn the whole story, I react based on my assumptions of what they intended. Often, this

How do you tend to react to negative information or unfavourable opinions about yourself?

....

....

....

....

can be embarrassing when I eventually learn their true intentions and how unfounded my reactions were. If I had been patient enough to wait and discover the whole story, I would have saved myself the angry emotions and some embarrassment.

Fortunately, now that I have noticed this pattern, I try to suspend judgement until I can talk in greater depth to the other person. Surprisingly, my initial reaction to the issue was often wrong or incomplete. When the other person explains, I see that part of my assumptions about their intentions were not as I had imagined. If I had walked away, accusing them unreasonably, I would have damaged the relationship based purely on my incorrect perceptions.

Next time you find yourself ready to react, pause long enough to evaluate the circumstances. Imagine what might have led to this event, how you may have been responsible, and the evidence of the other person's trustworthiness. Please pay attention to the circumstances that led the person to act as they did. Focus on seeking understanding and reconciling what you believe or feel with the complete information when you can. This information can only come by listening to their side of the story.

In the case study about political parties and candidates, the pastoral team at CCC helped the congregation delay their judgement of whom to vote for. They encouraged the community to investigate each candidate, asking: "Who is going to be a better leader and why?" and "What does their platform offer that is transformational and supportive to most people?" They could then vote (or withhold their votes) based on sound knowledge rather than other casual realities, such as their preference for a particular ethnicity, race, or gender.

Active Listening

To have enough information to help you change your mind, you need to understand the other person's position. How many times have you talked with someone and only later realized that they did not understand what you were saying, or in the case of a conflict, they took your words and twisted them to support their position? Have you done the same to others?

Understanding the other person can only happen through active listening or intentional listening for understanding. What we mean by listening here is a deliberate effort to hear and understand the other individual. The desire is to fully understand their positions, needs, or intentions and, where possible, to act on the new information.

The art of active listening requires not only full attentiveness to the other person but also open communication. To engage fully, you need to tune out all distractions. Distractions can be internal, such as your preconceived ideas and perceptions, but can also be external – in other words, things in the context that take your full attention away from proper engagement with the other person.

The rising occurrence of distracting stimuli around us, especially technologies, are dangers to good listening. All around us, things cry out for our attention, from cell phones to music to videos. Can you think of times you have wanted to have an in-depth conversation with someone else, but they were glued to their phone, tablet, computer, TV, or radio?

I am guilty too. I often assume I can be on social media or watch TV while also having an intelligent conversation with someone right in front of me. Picking up the phone, checking social media, or watching TV in the middle of a conversation is often culturally accepted in some communities. Many of us believe the myth that we can multitask. But research shows that technology and interruptions are detrimental to deep concentration and action. It is impossible to be distracted and yet engaged enough to understand the other entirely. These are not just annoyances. They are real hindrances to authentic communication. We must intentionally avoid them whenever we want to understand the other person, especially in a serious conversation such as trying to handle a conflict.

My friend would confront her husband with a request to talk about a sticky issue, but he often found excuses not to engage. She would then bring things up in the evening. He repeatedly argued that after work he wanted to watch the news or a favourite TV show. This became his go-to habit, and the family accumulated many unresolved issues over time.

It took my friend working with a counsellor to convince her husband to take time for in-depth conversations without the TV or technology. The best way to do this was to plan their meetings, typically for sometime over the weekend. As a result, they found that their conversations were deeper, and they could address their needs without undue accumulation.

As my friend found, if you are trying to communicate something important, it is best done when both parties can silence distractions and put them aside. I know, for example, not to call my Kenyan friends at 9 p.m. because almost everyone is glued to the news on TV at that hour. If I want undivided attention, I will call before then, keep my conversation short, and never go beyond that sacred time. Many people habitually leave the TV on, even when no one is watching. Sometimes this is so loud that it competes with conversations. On a few occasions, I have been frank enough to request my hosts to turn off the TV so that we can talk.

Once external distractions have been removed, intentional or active listening still involves a conscious decision to pay attention to someone else's communication to better understand the issues and the other person's intentions. Allow the other person time to explore their ideas, thoughts, and expressions. As they do, pay keen attention without interrupting or countering their message. This goes beyond just hearing the other's words, to deeply understanding the person's feelings, underlying motives, core concerns, and point of view.

Let's look at a few skills that communication experts consider essential for active listening: body language, open-ended questions, and paraphrasing. While not every skill applies to every conversation, the more skills you learn, the better your understanding of others.

Body language

Experts argue that over 90 per cent of our face-to-face communication is non-verbal. Whatever we do with our bodies during communication is thus crucial to understanding. The body language of both the communicator and the receiver of the message matters. Body postures like appropriate gestures, smiling, nodding, and other agreeable facial expressions communicate attentiveness and agreement. Eye contact and touch can also be powerful, but that may also depend on culture as to when these are acceptable. Looking away, frowning, crossing your arms, grunting, and sighing could communicate being guarded or disagreeing with the speaker.

Follow-up with open-ended questions

Asking questions of the speaker helps clarify what you heard and if that is what they intended. But these questions need to be open-ended, as opposed to those questions that require only "yes" or "no" answers, or questions that seem to discount or shut down the speaker. Open-ended questions invite further clarification. An example would be, "I hear what you are saying about my listening. Tell me more. How could that improve?"

Paraphrase

Paraphrasing what you heard helps clarify the message and is an active way to stay engaged with the speaker. When you mirror back to the other person what they said, they feel reassured that you have been paying attention and have heard them. They feel cared for. This can bring emotional closeness and shift the tone of the conversation. An example of paraphrasing could be, "Let me see if I understand what you are saying. You went to his house with a proposal to be business partners, and he was evasive in his response. Is that right?"

Conclusion

Kirwa, the Southside leader, interrupted the argument between Milka and Mr Ngoni. He said, "I think it's time to begin our study for today. For the next six weeks, all the church home groups will work through a discussion guide to explore the issues arising from the sermons. As group leaders, we have been trained to set ground rules for our time together. We encourage members to come to the meetings with an open mind and a willingness to learn. We want to focus on sharing factual rather than unverified information and talking with each other without becoming emotional. We also want to avoid abusive language and mischaracterizing the candidates and their followers. I think we can do this together. Are we all on board?"

The first few weeks of the Southside's discussions were challenging, and it proved hard to engage in honest conversations. But as the senior pastor's preaching and the group leader encouraged the members, they discussed the various perspectives openly. Many members appreciated the honesty in bringing these issues to the fore.

At the end of the series, Kirwa, asked if Milka and Mr Ngoni would be open to revisiting their conversation using an exercise in the discussion guide. Encouraged by the newly created open culture, they agreed. Kirwa reminded them of the principles of active listening: "Each person will take turns asking open-ended questions of each other. Don't interrupt or respond with your own opinions. Are you ready?"

They nodded, and Milka began. "Mr Ngoni, help me understand your perspective. Why do you think your candidate will lead well?"

"For me, it's about the person's experience and expertise. He is more qualified and has led a large international NGO."

"But how do you connect your faith with your voting?"

"To me, it's worse to have someone claiming to be a Christian and suspected of corruption than to have a non-Christian in power."

Milka was tempted to cut in with the lack of evidence again, but she kept quiet and nodded to encourage Mr Ngoni to continue.

"You wouldn't believe how many supposedly Christian colleagues I've had ask for kickbacks in business. It's a constant fight to be a person of integrity – and I have managed. But when I try to evangelize my non-Christian colleagues, they always point to poor leaders claiming to be Christians. To me, the church's credibility and witness are at stake when we promote leaders tainted with corruption scandals."

The leader spoke up. "Great job – thank you both. Mr Ngoni, it's now your turn to ask a question."

"All right. Milka, why do you think your candidate will be a good leader?"

"It's like I said before. He stands for Christian values and family values that our country needs."

"What values are you talking about?"

"You know . . . strong marriages and sexual purity – the obvious ones that you and I took for granted when we were growing up."

Mr Ngoni decided to try paraphrasing. "So, you feel the country's morals are becoming looser."

"You wouldn't believe what I see in the schools I teach. The things that come out of their mouths! They are just kids, but they are exposed to pornography on cell phones. More parents are divorced than I have ever seen before. Now can you imagine when they force me to teach that new curriculum? They want to mislead and confuse children. How can I even stay in my post as a teacher when I know what it will do to our country?"

Kirwa said, "All right, this next part of the exercise is affirmations. Each of you will share something you appreciate about the other person's perspective or an area of common ground."

Milka said, "Mr Ngoni cares about evangelism more than I realized."

Mr Ngoni said, "We both care about integrity and the direction in which our country is heading."

By the end of the exercise, Milka and Mr Ngoni still disagreed on who would do a better job as a leader and which policies were necessarily the best for the country. But, with Kirwa's help, Milka and Ngoni heard each other's side and changed their mind about each other. Instead of seeing each other as enemies, they realized that the other person was also a responsible citizen able to have a healthy debate on various possibilities.

It is good to change your mind when you have new information or insights that lead you to reconsider your positions or decisions. Changing one's mind is not an admission of folly but a mark of wisdom. The Bible and many cultures teach us that humility is a wise way to protect and grow our relationships.

Changing one's mind is part of developing a growth mindset, a learning attitude that believes there is always room to improve and learn, and that, in turn, has been proven to foster better outcomes. This takes effort, such as training yourself to listen to others and to speak in ways that heal the relationship. Of course, ensuring that changes are based on sound reasoning rather than just impulsiveness is important. We will, however, find that flexibility and willingness to grow help nurture our relationships.

> **What do you do that may get in the way of active listening? Ask someone else close to you to help you assess this. What could you do to develop your listening and communication skills?**
>
> ....
> ....
> ....
> ....
> ....
> ....
> ....
> ....
> ....

Group Discussion

1. Discuss statements or proverbs from your community that encourage holding off rash judgement and allow a willingness to change your mind. On the other hand, what elements of your culture discourage people from applying these?

2. What barriers does your family have to communicating well? I mentioned a loud television in the background or the couple whose weeknights were too busy to talk. What practices do you have or could you implement to make communicating easier?

9

No Piles Please!

> *Charovedzera charovedzera; gudo rakakwira mawere kwasviba* (SHONA, ZIMBABWE).
>
> "One who is used to something is one who is used to something; the baboon climbed the precipice in the dark."
> **MEANING:** We do easily that to which we are accustomed.

M hiripiri (Piri, as his friends call him) fell into bad luck when his business kiosk burned down. Many of the community members came to his aid.

However, a rumour began to spread that Piri burned his kiosk down for that very purpose: to get help from the community. As the story spread, some community members chose not to help. When Piri heard the rumours, he was distraught. But he suspected who might be behind them: Tendai, his childhood friend.

Piri and Tendai had grown up together in the same village. Before moving to the city, they ran a joint business in the town close to the village. Unfortunately, things did not go well, and the venture failed. They went their different ways without sorting out their responsibilities for the failed partnership. Although they were both able to move past the financial losses, they treated each other with suspicion. Piri believed he was a gentleman and prided himself as a good friend and caregiver. But Tendai knew Piri better than most people and did not think so.

As fate would have it, they ended up in the same part of the capital city. They often ran into each other at tribal celebrations where communities preserve their language and customs. They also played football over the weekends at the community grounds at the edge of town. The next time Piri saw Tendai at the football field, he decided to confront him.

"*Shamwari* [friend], what is this rumour I hear you are spreading about me?"

"What are you accusing me of now?" Tendai replied.

"That I burned my own kiosk. How could you possibly think I would ever do that?"

"*Mukoma wangu* [my brother]," Tendai said, drawing closer to Piri, "why would I spread those kinds of rumours? We have been friends since birth. Even though we have had our differences, I have been at your side. Indeed, I was the first to offer you help after this terrible ordeal. I am sad that you would suspect me this way."

"Are you saying that these stupid rumours did not arise with you?"

"They absolutely did not!"

Piri was confused. He was sure it had been Tendai who had spread the rumours. But, of course, it's not as if Tendai would admit to it if he had.

Many of us have been in Piri and Tendai's shoes. We cross swords with a neighbour or colleague at work, and they stop talking to us. Something else goes wrong – as it always does – and one of us quickly brings up the break in the past. Distrust and suspicion reveal that the past issue is unresolved and continues to affect us today.

Sadly, holding on to past injuries in this way hinders our ability to develop new positive experiences with others. In this chapter, we look at how to avoid letting issues build up, and how to let go of grudges, forgive, and move on as soon as possible. We want to live in the present, not be stuck in the past.

When a Good Memory Is a Bad Thing

When my sons were younger, they often had conflicts with each other. One was good at "remembering everything," while his brother was good at "forgetting everything". If an issue arose between them, the "remembering" brother would bring up issues that happened months or even years back to prove that his brother was acting in malice. But his brother did not wish to remember anything, especially when he was the offending party. Teaching them the balance was a long and insightful process. One needed to learn to lay off with the history, while his brother needed to learn not to repeat the hurt towards his brother.

We often lump past issues together to tell a story, often negative. We interpret the current hurt as part of something the other person intentionally does to hurt us, or a pattern that shows their intentions are evil and that they always do the wrong thing. When we bring up history, we often conflate the problem. Compounding is often used to control the narrative and the other person.

There are aggressive and passive ways of allowing the past to dictate your relationship and its future. Aggressive defensiveness may show up as overt confrontation, criticizing the other person, or listing accusations. On the passive side, people give each other the silent treatment. They may withdraw, disengage, and withhold intimacy. They likely still list the hurts, but mentally rather than out loud. All these communicate to the other that they are less-than, which can be a terrible means of controlling them. But, in reality, their current behaviour and the future of the relationship are being controlled by the past.

Memorizing and constantly recalling every hurt shows immaturity and lack of goodwill. It suggests that the other party is either insidious or incapable of change. It can communicate that you think you have a better handle on the issues in question or that you are more objective and righteous. However, if we are honest, we usually recognize that we also have our past mistakes, and so do they.

In contrast, love "does not demand its own way. It is not irritable, and it keeps no record of being wronged" (1 Corinthians 13:5). Are you keeping a record of wrongs? Perhaps you have heard someone say, "forgive but do not forget" – a common attitude in our society. In contrast to biblical wisdom, we want to hang on to offence and remind people of their evil, or, at the very least, be sure to avoid them so that they never hurt us again.

Sometimes, we bring issues to a conflict that are not necessarily related to the other person. As we discussed in a previous chapter, our perceptions of the other person can be affected by our suspicions or stereotypes of a group. Or perhaps the situation reminds us of another situation with someone else and we assume it will end up the same way.

Many societies have generational wounds and the memories to go with them. As mentioned earlier, growing up, I was instructed that people from a neighbouring clan were our enemies. No one knew the real issues; we just knew not to deal with them and that we could never marry them. My agemates from the other side were taught the same thing. We treated each other with suspicion and rarely shared in anything – besides the enmity.

In my travels worldwide, I have encountered the same enduring myths about groups hating each other. What surprises me is that current generations often have no idea where the break started.

Antagonists on both sides have crafted stories and stereotypes as reasons for the hostility. For example, I travelled to the Republic of Georgia soon after Russia had occupied the Eastern part of the country in an internationally condemned conflict. Our ethnic Georgian host had some ugly things to say about Russians. I also spent some time with ethnic Russians living in Georgia who had stories to support their side. The two groups with similar ancestry have occupied the region for centuries and have even intermarried. Unfortunately, they also have memories of injury. The issues are no longer apparent, but rehashing the history reinforces the hatred and boundaries.

This is why the Bible warns against bitterness, which is when our anger simmers for so long that we are tempted to act on it against others. Unforgiveness only grows bigger with time, driving a wedge deeper. Months or years later, people are no longer talking or they hate each other. Instead of love, enmity takes hold, destroying even the best relationships. It is what led Cain to kill his brother, Abel, and what leads to an escalating conflict spiral, as we discussed earlier.

Processing Past Pain

Of course, "keeping no record of wrongs" does not mean we totally ignore the past. Human memory is an integral part of our survival. It helps us avoid hurt and pain. There is nothing wrong with remembering the pain of a situation or the danger a problem once posed. What is important is how we allow that memory to affect our future.

The Sankofa symbol of the Akan of Ghana reminds them to learn from the past in order to inform both the present and the future. The symbol is a mythical bird walking forward but turning its head to reach back to what is left behind. We reach back to embrace the best of the past that can be applied today, but we have one foot planted in the present and one lifted towards the future. Rejecting getting stuck in past hurts is essential, and so is remembering what worked and was energizing and uplifting.

Many interpersonal relationships lead to heartaches, and many people who have been hurt this way are cautious and genuinely apprehensive about exploring other relationships. Past pain can make you afraid to let down your guard. You want to stay in control and are scared to let go of what you are comfortable with. To avoid being hurt again, we are tempted to avoid those who have hurt us. As a result, we build up defences to protect ourselves.

I am not saying that you should open yourself up to everyone in every manner possible. But unless you are willing to be vulnerable in some circumstances, you will not develop deeper relationships with people around you. Many people sabotage a relationship's growth because their baggage makes them afraid to open themselves up to the next person. The more defences someone has built over past relationships, the less investment and intimacy they have in a relationship, and the easier it becomes to avoid addressing problems when they find themselves in conflict.

Breaking defences is a challenging task. It takes courage to overcome the painful past and confidently give yourself to a new relationship. But if you get into a new relationship while still dealing

Think of a hurtful situation from the past. Write down any feelings you have about the situation when you think about it today.

. . . .

. . . .

. . . .

. . . .

with defences you've built around yourself, chances are that the new relationship's growth will be stunted.

By avoiding risk, people miss out on the joy of a true friendship or even a love relationship. Often you hear married couples complain, "He doesn't woo me any more" or "She doesn't sweep me off my feet." A dulled intimacy is often part of the cause. Maybe due to the couple's various experiences, either one or both stopped trying to do all they can to keep their relationship fresh. Add some conflict to their circumstances, and you may have a toxic mix that could significantly disrupt the relationship or even end it. Perhaps this is why keeping a record of wrongs is the opposite of love.

When we are not careful to address issues as they arise and keep them from piling up, past hurts can seep into current situations and complicate our relationships. Can you imagine how difficult it is, especially in loving relationships, when one treats the other based on what happened before – maybe even in another relationship? Of course, it would be ideal if we were always aware of why we react the way we do when in conflict. But we tend to react mostly subconsciously and only reflect on the real motives afterwards.

Proactively reflecting on and becoming aware of these past hurts help us to reduce their power to determine how we act today. Review some of your relationships to ensure you are not conflating things from one relationship with another. Whenever you get into a new relationship or conflict, consider what defences you might have built due to former interactions with this person or other people in your past. Are you allowing those experiences to colour your current relationship? What else might you be carrying? How might this impact your relationships now?

When dealing with people in a conflict, I ask them to tell me about any past issues that might impact the current situation and whether those are related. I am often surprised by how many different answers I get. I have learned that if you try to resolve the current issue while the problems from the past have not been adequately addressed, these can damage the relationship. Therefore, it is crucial to discover the real issues that led to a conflict and how to focus on the current moment. Work to resolve the current issue, forgive, and then move on.

Of course, it can be very hurtful having to deal with repeat offences. Often, it is best to have a conversation to establish the reasons behind repeated offences, intentional or unintentional. The reality of being connected to other humans is that we make mistakes. If these are repeated often, there may be a need for a deeper conversation, holding each other accountable, or involving a third party. But if this is a malicious act or a withdrawal that is intended to abuse and control, removing yourself from the situation is essential. Seek the intervention of authorities or others to save yourself. We will discuss this further in the next chapter.

Keep the Process Short and Positive

Have you been in situations where issues tend to drag on forever? When issues take a long time to be properly resolved, it is easy for other conflicts to pile up on top of them, making the situation even worse. It is like a motor accident in the middle of a busy road. If the cars are not moved off to the side, it will be easy for other vehicles to hit the stopped cars, causing a pile-up.

As much as possible, we need to keep the process of sorting through conflict short and not get bogged down in unnecessary delays. Grudges and bitterness can develop when hurtful situations linger. The time-lapse itself cannot be energizing to anyone in the relationship. The sooner we can come to terms with what happened, then offer and receive forgiveness, the soon we can move towards rebuilding or maintaining our relationships.

What if you find yourself in a situation where issues have already accumulated and begun to pile up? Remember how we discussed taking the initiative to save the relationship and doing "all that you can to live in peace with everyone"? Instead of dwelling on the other person's responsibility, the problem, or the hurt, focus on three things:

Focus on what you can do

Take the initiative and act purposely to address the issues, rather than wait for things to work out on their own, which rarely happens. If you do engage the other party, avoid blaming and shaming. Instead, find non-threatening and inviting ways to approach them. Find positive ways in which to steer the conversation. That may require finding a neutral place to meet or even a third party to help where necessary. Of course, starting with just the two of you is best before involving too many other people.

Focus on what you did

What issues are your responsibility, and how can you take care of those for the other party to feel comfortable acting similarly? For example, did you act or speak carelessly? Do you need to apologize for your mistakes? This might be an excellent place to start. It invites the other party to consider their role in the conflict and maybe act on their own transgressions. There are no guarantees that they will respond in kind, of course, but act on what is your responsibility anyway. In addition, understand that not all issues can actually be addressed. It takes humility to accept this reality, especially when dealing with contentious situations. You may need a clear understanding of what you can handle and be willing to take action.

Focus on a positive future

Handling conflicts and relationship breaks is draining. Repairing the cracks is rarely an easy process. Keep your motivation by focusing on the possibility of a restored relationship, or at least an understanding with the other party. A positive attitude does not mean being naïve and expecting that, when you act on your part, the other party is obligated to respond in kind. They may not be interested in re-engaging. However, if you don't approach the situation with a positive attitude, you may be tempted to give up when the situation becomes heated or does not play out as quickly as you expected.

Making Peace with Others Brings Peace with God

Focusing on what *you* can do is not my idea; it is biblical. Jesus teaches in the New Testament: "So if you are presenting a sacrifice at the altar in the Temple and you suddenly remember that someone has something against you, leave your sacrifice there at the altar. Go and be reconciled to that person. Then come and offer your sacrifice to God" (Matthew 5:23-24).

The first lesson this teaches us is that whatever your acts of devotion, you cannot be at peace with God when you are not at peace with others. Some people do not care much about their relationships because "they are in right standing with God." They may think of any reaction to their poor behaviour as a "persecution" they are willing to endure. We also have people committing atrocities against others in the name of God. These so-called fundamentalists will harm others because of their devotion to their religion and God.

The teachings of Jesus show that this is not possible; you cannot truly love and serve God when you are unloving or hurtful to those around you. Jesus teaches, "Love each other. Just as I have loved you, you should love each other. Your love for one another will prove to the world that you are my disciples" (John 13:34-35). Look at how Christ handles those around him, with gentleness and respect for his followers, and stern warnings for those who oppose and seek his demise. He forgives even his enemies, because they do not know what they are doing (Luke 23:34). He is against their arrogance and the evil that binds them, but he does not hate them. In a world that promotes "getting even", a different standard of love marks the Christian.

Another thing to notice in the Matthew 5 passage is that the perpetrator is taking the initiative to clear things up. They have hurt someone who is now angry with them, so they need to go to the person they have hurt and smooth things out. This way, they can come back and worship God without any baggage. Jesus teaches that the most significant commands are to love God and to love others as oneself (Matthew 22:37-40). The true essence of life and true worship involve good relationships with God and fellow humans.

I saw this principle lived out after a nasty break with a good colleague who was also a friend. We had come out on opposite sides on an issue in the office. I viewed his ideas as untenable. I had spent time researching this issue and felt our team would be best served considering different views before moving forward.

He, on the other hand, presented his side as the only decision for the team. He used his bombastic personality to drive the decision to his ideas, leaving no room for alternatives or for me to challenge his views. The team adopted his suggestion, and we were quickly on our way to implementing this new project. I left the meeting in frustration, vowing to keep my ideas to myself and scale back our friendship. Who has a friend that does not listen to them and instead uses their personality to drive their agendas?

As it turns out, my colleague was the better man. Although I did not voice it, he noticed that he had hurt me. A few months later, he invited me for coffee and a conversation. At first, I was reluctant, but

I attended the meeting to honour him. In his wisdom, he steered the discussion in ways that slowly helped me to lower my guard. When I brought up my disappointment, he apologized for the hurt without making any excuses. As a result of his efforts to reconcile, I simply could not hold on to my disappointment with a clear conscience. I thus agreed to drop the matter and focus on our future relationship. We are still friends years later.

We need more people like my friend – people who seek peace with others, together with their worship of God. For perpetrators, that looks like taking the initiative to apologize and reconcile. But for people who are wronged, their willingness to let go of bitterness is also an important part of their worship of God. That is why Jesus goes so far as to say, "If you forgive those who sin against you, your heavenly Father will forgive you. But if you refuse to forgive others, your Father will not forgive your sins" (Matthew 6:14-15). Let's look at practical ways in which we can apologize and forgive, whichever side of an argument we find ourselves on.

Repentance and Forgiveness

How do you let go of the unresolved issues that hold your relationships back? You repent when you have offended others and forgive when you are offended.

Repentance is more than a causal acknowledgement of the wrong or harm caused. You need to own what you did. True repentance is not just saying, "Sorry." It means taking responsibility for the trust broken and the hurt caused – whether by your words or actions (or lack of them). Don't make any excuses for mistakes made, but fully accept the other person's pain. No wonder it takes humility and acceptance of failure to really repent.

Forgiveness is releasing the other person from having to pay for the hurt caused. Think of damage in terms of debt. Each debt must

> **Here are some ways in which to offer an appropriate apology. Can you think of others?**
>
> 1. Genuinely and openly accept your error, personal responsibility, and its results.
> 2. Don't blame or accuse the other, either directly or indirectly for your mistakes.
> 3. Offer to repay or make up for any damage caused.
> 4. Request but do not demand forgiveness.
> 5. Ask God for forgiveness and to remove your guilt.

be paid by someone. If you lean on a cabinet at my house, and it topples, breaking my prized dishes, I can make you pay to replace the broken pieces, or I can let it go and pay to replace those pieces myself. When a friend breaks trust by saying something offensive, the process of healing that needs to occur is a type of cost, a debt of love and trust. We cannot just ignore the debt as if it never happened. Instead of demanding they pay, breaking off the relationship or exacting a cost to maintaining the relationship, you may consider excusing them of the "payment".

In the best cases, repentance and forgiveness are a response to each other. You may confront a perpetrator in order to understand their wrong. They will acknowledge their wrong and seek forgiveness. They demonstrate their repentance by making restitution, a payment of the debt that tries to rectify the hurt or harm done. Since restitution does not usually fully compensate for the distress or harm caused, the victim still must choose to forgive and absorb some of the cost themselves.

However, in some cases, as a victim, you may choose to forgive the perpetrator even before they acknowledge their wrong. Even if they never apologize, you can choose to free yourself from the bondage of emotions such as anger, fear, and bitterness that holding on to a grudge induces.

Psychologist Everett Worthington has spent his career studying forgiveness. Emotional forgiveness is closely connected to physical and psychological benefits. He developed a five-step process to achieve emotional forgiveness using the acronym REACH:

- **R** – Recall the hurt. Review the situation and come to terms with the hurt perpetrated against you.

- **E** – Empathize with the one who hurt you. It may be difficult, but try to see the perpetrator as a victim themselves. Few people can rest easy after causing others pain. They too are hurting. Your forgiveness helps them in their process of healing.

- **A** – Altruistically give the gift of forgiveness. Forgiveness is an act of the will, whether the perpetrator acknowledges their evil or not. As a victim, it is up to you to offer that from a heart of grace.

- **C** – Commit to the forgiveness you offered. Determine not to hold a grudge against the perpetrator as you move forward.

- **H** – Hold on to forgiveness when you doubt. Forgiving does not mean an end to the hurt or to the other person wronging you again. It also does not guarantee that they will repay you for the hurt they caused (restitution). So, even if they are mean, determine to hold on to your resolution to forgive.[1]

Through Jesus's sacrifice, God shows us the importance of grounding our peacemaking and relationship-building on repentance and forgiveness. The mission of Jesus's life and death was to pay the debt of sin for all humanity. God was the aggrieved party, and evil

---

1 REACH Forgiveness of Others. © 2023 Everett Worthington | Designed and developed by ScienceSites: websites for scientists. Accessed July 15, 2023.

deprived humanity of a relationship with their creator God. This cost Jesus's life as a ransom for all (Matthew 20:28).

God's attitude of taking the initiative and absorbing the cost of the conflict is also amplified through other stories in the Bible. For example, Jacob, with the assistance of his mother, deceived his father and defrauded his brother, Esau, of his birthright. Esau was so angry that he wanted to kill Jacob, so Jacob ran off to hide for many years. When Jacob returned to claim his inheritance, Esau forgave Jacob, which transformed their relationship, despite not getting the estate back (Genesis 33). Esau overlooked a significant hurt to restore the relationship. When the brothers met, Jacob also offered gifts as restitution to reconcile with Esau.

Myths about Repentance and Forgiveness

Repentance and forgiveness are sometimes mistaken as being weak or frivolous. That is not the case at all. When Jesus forgives those killing him, he is not yielding to their power. He is exercising his freedom not to take revenge against them.

In many societies, encouragement to forgive can sometimes be fronted as the noble thing to do. The victim is almost coerced to "forgive and forget", sometimes by being made to feel guilty or even shamed. This is not forgiveness and should not be the way to address hurtful situations.

No one *must* forgive. Choosing to forgive is not weak, neither does it excuse the hurt. It is a bold choice. You decide what to do with the hurt and how you want to treat the person in the future. You prefer not to continue the hurts and hold on to bitterness. Forgiveness is not always easy or the quickest way out of a conflict. In most cases, it is one of the most challenging principles to master.

And that last line brings me to an important caveat. Just because you forgive does not mean you lay down like a doormat for people to walk over you whenever they wish. It means that you overcome their evil with good but do not submit to continued mistreatment. Especially if the other is unwilling to acknowledge their sin, you may do well to step back and let them move on with their business.

A very close friend invited me to join him in a donor-funded project. As a businessman, he could implement the plans well, but he did not have my expertise in NGO work or the specific grant area. For the grant to go through, the granting agency needed to see that he had a professional with experience and expertise.

So I joined him and even developed the proposal myself. In the budget, I included my consulting fees, which he would then pay me as agreed once the project was funded. Our discussions were cordial until the grant was fully funded.

He proceeded to delete my access to the shared document folder and instructed the project staff we had jointly hired not to respond to me. I was shocked. He would not return my calls or emails. Several months later, I saw online that he had replaced me with his sister, but he kept my information as the project consultant, which meant no pay for me. Because he was the principal applicant, he could argue that he had just replaced the roles within the grant and therefore did not have to pay me, the consultant.

List some examples of good and not-so-good apologies you have witnessed.

....
....
....
....
....

As you can imagine, I was enraged. However, I had no recourse. I could write to the donor and report my "friend". The project might then be cancelled, exposing his malice, but also denying benefits to the people in poverty it was intended to serve. I prayed and consulted with my wife. We agreed that fighting for my role and the pay due to me were not worth the possibility that the community would lose out. I sent my friend a letter, an email, and a voicemail, telling him I forgave him. I did not need him to pay me, even though that was the right thing to do. I only asked him to implement the project as envisioned for the sake of the people.

The project succeeded. Although I was not part of it, I was proud of my role in developing the proposal and applying for the grant using my credentials, which were key to winning the project money. I was also not bitter towards my friend, although unfortunately, given his devious behaviour and lack of response, we could not continue our friendship – his choice, not mine. It has been more than 10 years now that we have not talked. But if he called, I would take his call, although I might not lend a hand in a similar project.

The Power of Forgiveness

Forgiveness and repentance – though they are some of the most challenging principles we discuss – are also the most transformative. Even in deep betrayal and violence, they open the door to reconcile families and whole communities.

Consider the biblical story of Joseph and his brothers. You need to read the full story in Genesis to get all the twists and turns of this critical story. The summary is that Joseph's brothers sold him into slavery in Egypt out of jealousy and malice. Years later, they ended up in Egypt, trying to buy grain during a famine. By this time, Joseph had ascended to second-in-command in Egypt after a period in prison. Once he recognized them, he tempted and later revealed himself to them and forgave them.

But that was not the end of the matter. When their father, Jacob, who had moved to Egypt to escape the famine, died, the brothers brought up the past, thinking Joseph would remember and act harshly against them. They lied that their father had guaranteed their safety. They were still living with the guilt of having tried to kill Joseph. Joseph's response was the best pre-Christ forgiveness offer one can ever imagine:

> But Joseph replied, "Don't be afraid of me. Am I God, that I can punish you? You intended to harm me, but God intended it all for good. He brought me to this position so I could save the lives of many people. No, don't be afraid. I will continue to take care of you and your children." So he reassured them by speaking kindly to them (Genesis 50:19-21).

This was complete forgiveness of the past and a promise to the brothers to care for their descendants, something they had tried to deny Joseph.

Joseph also communicated to his brothers that his forgiveness was not earned or retractable. The offer for reconciliation he had made years earlier had been genuine. It had not been to appease them or their father. He was honestly living out of his faith in a God who "intended it all for good" (Genesis 50:20). That is the offer of forgiveness that we all receive from Christ, for all our sins, without any qualifications or the potential for losing it. Such a grand reconciliation and a transformation of our relationship with God!

Joseph was able to forgive his enemies because he saw what God had done for him. Jesus also teaches us to love our enemies (Luke 6:27-36), and the first step is to recognize the grace that God, in his tender mercy, has extended to us, his "enemies." We did not deserve this kind of treatment, but God did everything to win us back to him. Therefore, he asks us to do the same and not want to have enemies. The new life of the forgiven people means that we are members of the same family and so need to treat each other as such – even when it is the kind of family Joseph had.

Some amazing stories of forgiveness and reconciliation have also emerged years after the heinous atrocities committed in Rwanda. In the traditional Gacaca Community Courts for trying the guilty, the victims were invited to meet the perpetrators if they chose to. Some family members decided to go to the prison to forgive those who killed their relatives. The result is that the generational interpersonal/interfamily wounds were healed, and this helped birth a new chapter in interethnic relations.

In one case, a mother who lost an arm and suffered through the death of her baby chose to forgive the man who meted such evil against her. After serving jail time, the man returned and repented to the victim. They were reconciled, and afterwards, both engaged in a brickmaking business. They also lived in the same neighbourhood in which the crimes were committed. In another extreme case, a woman decided to marry the guy who had participated in the killing of her husband. That is an intense love for the enemy that I cannot imagine possible! While I am not promising (or necessarily recommending) that particular outcome, it shows us how radically transformational forgiveness and repentance can be.

Conclusion

Piri stepped away from Tendai, joining his other friends on the bench. "Tendai says he didn't start the rumour. But I learned my lesson long ago not to trust him."

Nyasha chimed in, "I know who started it, and it was not Tendai."

"You know who came up with this gossip?"

"I was there when that happened." Nyasha said. "It was Obed, the guy in the sweatshirt over there. The other day, we were at Colonel, the bar on the corner. He asked, 'Could Piri have burned down his kiosk so that we support him?' I think some guys in the bar thought it was fact. But Obed was drunk. It's stupid, bro. You should just ignore it."

Piri walked back over to Tendai. He placed his hand on his shoulder and apologized, "Please forgive me, Shamwari. I am sorry. With our past, I often think that we are like bulls with locked horns, if you know what I mean."

"All good, Mukoma wangu. I know we have stuff we need to work through, but please know I think highly of you and would not make up such a nasty story about you," Tendai said.

"It has been tough for me, and these falsehoods are like salt on an open wound."

"You know, I don't want you suspecting me whenever something goes wrong. Maybe we need to revisit our issues."

Piri sighed. "Okay. Yes, I suppose it is time. But not right now. We have a football game to play."

We are often tempted to dredge the past for problems that serve only to compound the current situation. Maybe you have seen this in long-term relationships like married couples! Unfortunately, all this does is muddy the waters further. When an attitude or belief is not confronted and corrected at the time, it can lead to more profound mistrust and misunderstanding, entrenching the conflict. When there have been genuine hurts in the past, and no apology or repentance has been sought, those injuries can morph into scars that one remembers when another conflict arises.

We need to leave the past in the past! To do this, we need to keep the issues current – in other words, address the cause of the current conflict and not pile on a heap of other issues from the past. We also need to practise offering and receiving apologies and repentance in order to renew the relationship on an ongoing basis. That is the true meaning of turning the other cheek!

Think of a situation where someone else hurt you. Use the REACH model to map out the process of forgiveness below. What would each of these steps look like or involve for you?

R Recall the hurt:

. . . .

. . . .

. . . .

E Empathize with the one who hurt you

. . . .

. . . .

. . . .

A Altruistically give the gift of forgiveness

. . . .

. . . .

. . . .

C Commit to the forgiveness you offered

. . . .

. . . .

. . . .

H Hold on to forgiveness when you doubt

. . . .

. . . .

. . . .

Group Discussion

1. What are the cultural expectations for repentance and forgiveness in your context? How appropriate are these expectations? What is good about them and what is wrong about them?

2. Confession is good for the soul. If you are willing, share with the group (or a close friend if you are reading the book alone) a hurtful situation that has not been resolved. After working through this chapter, what are you learning about how to approach this situation? Depending on your comfort level, invite the group to help with your thinking.

10

No More Cheeks to Turn

> *Adui wa mtu ni mtu* (Swahili, East Africa).
> "The enemy of a person is a person."
> **Meaning:** People are capable of abusing others.

Ojai was a government official who had risen from district officer to provincial commissioner. In his career, spanning over 30 years, he had rubbed shoulders with many influential individuals in the country, including some of the wealthiest businesspeople and politicians. He counted a former vice president among his personal friends.

In a recent change of government, the colonial provincial structures were replaced by a new structure of government. The new government offered Ojai and his colleagues early retirement. This took away a lot more than a job from him. The position of provincial commissioner came with many perks: official cars, servants, and the power to apportion public resources. Ojai had taken advantage of his office to acquire some properties this way. Although this is considered corruption, all government officials and politicians were doing it, and with the right signatures, specific properties could become private property. Ojai argued that if he did not take these properties himself, they would end up in the hands of others, many of whom were even more corrupt than he was.

Public outcry against corruption prompted the new government to do a wealth audit of all government officials and investigate all corruption cases. Ojai's name featured prominently in the preliminary report alleging corruption. He was summoned to appear before an ethics committee investigating these claims, where he denied all the accusations.

Ojai maintained publicly that he was innocent, but privately, he was scared. He knew that there was no legitimate way to justify all his wealth. In desperation, his wife introduced him to an influential pastor she had been following whose TV ministry attracted millions every week. Because of the pastor's increasing influence, Ojai was happy to befriend him, and confessed in confidence to the pastor. He owned up to the deals the government was investigating and much more that he had privately acquired through his position. With time, the pastor was able to curry some favours with members of the new government, and the investigations against Ojai were eventually dropped.

As their relationship blossomed, the pastor started making demands of Ojai. He borrowed vast sums of money and used Ojai's cars for long cross-country trips claiming that he was going on God's missions. He would return the cars without service or repairs when they broke down. The pastor would continually tell Ojai and his wife that they would be blessed for tithing their resources. Ojai emptied the family savings account to lend money to the pastor, who promised to repay whenever the ministry was able to.

Several months after, without consulting Ojai, the pastor announced on TV that he had led Ojai to Christianity and claimed that all his past sins had been forgiven. The broadcast of his testimony upset Ojai, but he was not able to contradict the pastor, given the preacher's vast following and public influence.

When Ojai tried to request repayment of the borrowed cash, the pastor was elusive, even jokingly suggesting Ojai should donate this amount to the cause of the gospel. He occasionally brought up Ojai's confession, saying that Ojai should be thankful that his case was dismissed following the pastor's personal intervention. Ojai's family was struggling financially now that he was unemployed. Ojai's wife was increasingly upset, demanding they end the relationship with the pastor. She stopped going to his church. This led to a strain on Ojai and his wife's relationship. Ojai felt trapped. He could not just walk away because the threats from the pastor to report his misdeeds would then be taken seriously and investigations against Ojai may even be reinstated.

Is It Abuse?

The questions posed in the previous chapters helped determine what route to pursue in a normal conflict situation. Those questions asked whether the issues were essential and possible to address, in which case steps could be taken in approaching the other party to engaging in a resolution process. If resolution did not seem likely or essential, the best action might be to hold off or separate, even if for the short term, until such a time when it might be feasible to re-engage. These conflict processes can lead to learning, growth, and transformation of the relationship.

However, this chapter assesses whether abuse is present, which leads to determining the best means to stop or end the relationship. Most relationships, especially intimate ones, are kind and support each party's development. These healthy relationships are characterized by mutual respect, trust, and even love, where appropriate. However, some relationships involve fear-based and controlling behaviour, threats, and even harmful attacks – all of which are forms of abuse. Abuse can sometimes be dangerous, with people hurting or even killing spouses or those who were once close friends.

The Gale Encyclopedia of Medicine defines abuse as "any action that intentionally harms or injures another person."[1] Abuse can take many forms, including direct and indirect forms of aggression. Although the following does not cover every type of abuse, a few examples include:

- physical abuse, such as assault, beating, or restraints, often by someone stronger;
- psychological abuse, which is mental control through acts like manipulation, blackmail, lying, or intimidation, or emotional control such as public shunning, acts of racism and sexism, and so forth;
- sexual abuse, which is manipulation or forceful engagement in any sexual activity without one's consent;
- verbal abuse, which may involve berating, insults, accusations, threats, blaming, or shaming; and
- depriving people, whether by isolating them, controlling their access to resources, or denying their needs so that they depend on the abuser in ways that are unhealthy.

Since the forms and layers of abuse can be varied, and we often have assumptions or stereotypes about what abuse looks like, some abuses are harder to spot than others. The psychological/emotional abuses are particularly difficult to spot, especially when they occur in intimate power-imbalanced relationships.

Abusive relationships often develop when one party has significant power over the other. However, anger and uncooperativeness could

---

1 Jacqueline L. Longe, ed., *The Gale Encyclopedia of Medicine*, 3rd ed. (Detroit, MI: Gale Group, 2006), s.v. "Abuse".

be a way someone with less power can also control the party with more power over them.

How do you know whether you are in a normal conflict or in an abusive situation? Psychotherapist and abuse survivor Anita Bentata compares emotional abuse with arguments:

> Abuse involves an environment and pattern of denial, punishment, fear and control, which systematically denies one person's reality, feelings, needs and differences. Whereas, arguments and conflict may involve someone denying another person's feelings or opinions in the moment, but you are not in fear of them or of consequences, and it is not embedded within a systematic process of control and denial.[2]

Another difference is that abuse is usually one-sided, with one person controlling the other or always getting their way. In contrast, normal conflict involves engaging each other with no clear power dynamic.[3] A few examples of what this control may look like are provided in the bulleted list in the sidebar.[4]

As an extreme example, many human trafficking cases are successful because the trafficker has undue power over the victim. They might initially lure their victim through incentives (e.g., a job or a better life), appealing to the victim's needs (e.g., being jobless), and promising to help. However, when the perpetrators have removed their victims from the environment where the victims have limited agency, they

2 Anita Bentata, "How to recognise the difference between conflict and Domestic Violence," LinkedIn.com, February 12, 2017, https://www.linkedin.com/pulse/how-recognise-difference-between-conflict-domestic-violence-bentata/. Accessed July 15, 2023.

3 "Is It Normal Conflict or Abuse?", Wevorce.com, October 14, 2016, https://www.wevorce.com/blog/is-it-normal-conflict-or-abuse/. Accessed July 15, 2023.

4 Crystal Raypole, "Understanding the Cycle of Abuse," Healthline.com, accessed April 6, 2023, https://www.healthline.com/health/relationships/cycle-of-abuse#takeaway.

strip them of their ability to defend themselves and control their circumstances. This can be through taking their travel documents away, withholding all contact with the outside world, and making the victim dependent on them for survival. In all these cases, what is common is that the victim has little or no power against their abuser.

More commonly, though, are abuses carried out in everyday relationships. For example, people in authority may leverage their positions to inflict pain and gain an advantage against others. We have all heard sad stories of junior staff members, especially women, being taken advantage of sexually by their supervisors. In these cases, the perpetrator uses his power over the victim's job security to force that person to sleep with him or do his bidding.

Often, abuse is committed by someone who knows the victim, with the most common abuses happening within families. When perpetrated against a spouse or partner, this is known as intimate partner abuse or domestic abuse. It can also include sexual assault

Abusive partners may often try to maintain control in the following ways:

- making all the decisions in the relationship
- controlling your words and behaviour
- keeping you from going to work, spending time with friends or loved ones, or seeing your healthcare provider
- threatening pets and children
- destroying belongings
- blaming you for their behaviour
- taking or controlling your money
- pressuring you to have sex
- going through your phone, computer, and personal belongings

and other forms of cruelty meted out against the partner who can do little to defend themself. Unfortunately, many millions stay in those abusive relationships, and no action is taken. They are either in powerless relationships with their perpetrators or, in other cases, this situation may be condoned as part of acceptable cultural and economic realities.

Gender-based violence is a form of abuse where one's gender is the reason for the power dynamic. Because women and girls may be physically weaker and often have less social power, this can happen to girls and women in a family, workplace, school, or elsewhere, using any of the forms of abuse in the sidebar on page 195 to harm the other.

All forms of abuse are unacceptable, and all people of goodwill need to do all they can to end any abuse wherever it is found.

Identify Abuse

So how do you recognize abuse, and what steps do you need to take to stop it? Here is a set of questions that help identify whether abuse might be happening:

- Is there a repeated pattern of mistreatment and violating my boundaries?
- Do I feel unsafe or uneasy around this person?
- Am I afraid the person will harm me if I do not do what they ask?
- Has the person threatened me?
- Has the person intentionally caused me harm or distress?
- Is there a power dynamic in the relationship?
- Is this relationship based on controlling or illegal behaviour?
- Is our relationship based on trust and free will, or am I under coercion?

- Are my safety and well-being at risk if the situation continues?
- Are my safety and well-being at risk if I confront the other party?
- Can I leave this relationship at will if I choose?[5]

1. A colleague at work confides in you that her father-in-law calls her often to demand money. He does not call his son, her husband. She is scared to tell her husband because he is not on talking terms with his dad. Is this abuse? Why or why not?

   . . . .

   . . . .

   . . . .

2. Your boss loses his temper at a department meeting and starts to hurl insults at a colleague he dislikes. Is this abuse? Why or why not?

   . . . .

   . . . .

   . . . .

3. You are walking in town and a stranger comments on your clothing. Is this abuse? Why or why not?

   . . . .

   . . . .

   . . . .

---

5 Adapted from: "Is It Normal Conflict or Abuse?", Wevorce.com, October 14, 2016, https://www.wevorce.com/blog/is-it-normal-conflict-or-abuse/ and from Crystal Raypole, "Understanding the Cycle of Abuse," Healthline.com, accessed April 6, 2023, https://www.healthline.com/health/relationships/cycle-of-abuse#takeaway.

Let's look at a situation to determine whether it is abusive. Imagine a husband who is an introverted engineer and quite wealthy. On the other hand, the wife is an extroverted lawyer. The two are doing very well by the country's standards. At least, that's what we all see from the outside. They own several properties, and their children go to elite private schools in the city. And the couple are also leaders in the local church.

After being married for 12 years, the wife expresses a desire to leave the relationship because she does not feel her partner is the best husband she "could have had." Their relationship worsens when the wife demands that she see other men whenever she wants. After pursuing these relationships for a couple of years, to her husband's chagrin, she leaves him for another man. This is infidelity, mistreatment, and heartless betrayal. However, we need more information to determine whether the wife's behaviour is controlling or whether there is a clear power dynamic for this to technically be abuse.

Suppose, though, that the husband is a refugee from a neighbouring country without proper immigration papers. Due to a broken immigration system that does not allow refugees to become citizens, he depends on his wife for his status. However, although the wife could help secure his status, she refuses to sign the papers for him confirming their marriage for many years. He does all his work under the table for one of his wife's relatives, and any time he tries to stand up for himself in the relationship, she reminds him that she could always tell her relative to end his employment. She insults him and has the final say in every dispute. Since the accounts and properties are all in her name, she controls his spending. If she were to leave him, he would be desperate, having no proper immigration status to fall back on. Afraid to go to the courts, he would lose all the property to his ex-wife. This is clearly an abusive situation. This, however, is a rather unusual story because, in many

> **List out some ways you have seen abuse in your community.**
>
> ....
>
> ....
>
> ....
>
> ....
>
> ....

contexts, it is often the husband who is the mistreating party. But more cases are coming out now where the opposite is true.

What Should You Do?

You may be asking, what if my answers to most or all the above questions confirm that I may be in an abusive relationship? What do I do next? Do I break off the relationship? What steps do I need to take to protect myself and possibly to get justice? These are not easy questions to answer. Much of it depends on the state of your relationship and other conditions you find yourself in.

In an abusive situation, your safety is the most important. As soon as possible, remove yourself from the situation and seek safety for yourself (and dependants like children). In such situations, it is always best to seek safety over ongoing understanding, especially when the person with authority has used power to undermine or abuse another.

In many situations, an abusive person has cut off the victim's options for escape. When there are power imbalances, the victim may be unable to change their circumstances. Or the laws are inadequate to protect the victims, even where abuse has been proven, such as in cases of gender-based violence. Perhaps the victim fears public shame and shunning if they leave the job that provides for their relatives. A child is, for example, at the mercy of a guardian or caregiver to avoid hunger or homelessness. A boyfriend might threaten his girlfriend's physical safety or even her life. An abusive husband might cut off all his wife's relationships, refusing to allow her to see her friends or family, currying favour with the pastor, or sowing lies among her relatives so that no one will believe her if she reaches out for help.

This is why seeking help is often the first step. Find someone trustworthy who will listen to you, provide a safe place to stay, provide for your physical needs, help you find a counsellor, or help you take your case to the authorities.

Suppose you are in an abusive situation but trying to repair a relationship or even pursue justice. In that case, you may be putting yourself in an environment where you could be hurt or further taken advantage of. The search for justice is tricky because not all parties have the same leverage to pursue the issues as equals. Secondly, you may risk additional injury when confronting an abuser in a position of power, especially if they have been known to take advantage of their position. It is never wise to put yourself in danger when seeking peace, even when working through a conflict with an equal party where there is no abuse present.

Assume that confronting the other party alone is not safe. When confronting the other party is necessary, it is best if the confrontation is made in the presence of another party (such as a mediator or a law-enforcement officer) and never by yourself, especially if you have been a victim before. While this book emphasizes the importance of transforming relationships, there can be a tendency to try to repair the relationship too early in abuse scenarios. Cultural pressure can also guilt-trip people into re-engaging with the perpetrator when it is unsafe to do so, such as when a woman is fleeing an abusive husband.

Until the perpetrator has experienced significant consequences, they will have little motivation to change and the victim is likely to end up experiencing abuse again.

Imagine a boss and subordinates in a hierarchical office. The boss has more power, which is sometimes abused in ways that make the relationship within the office abusive. Suppose the boss often berates, attacks, or threatens the subordinates. If the subordinates stand up for themselves, the boss's character is such that the boss might try to sabotage the subordinates' relationships with other people in the workplace, their career, or their job security. At this point, there is no hope of reconciliation or establishing a good relationship. It may be best to look for another job or start one's own business if possible. Reporting the situation to someone with more power may be a good option, but preferably only once they are in a position of safety.

In other contexts, we may face circumstances where we need to demand justice. Protesting injustices, corruption, abuses by the powerful, and so forth are ways to seek that justice, but we need to be wise in determining the best way to agitate or secure justice safely.

While the best advice is to seek safety and, possibly, justice, this may take much courage and even perhaps intervention by others. Nobody wants to have to choose between justice and safety. Still, sometimes it's necessary to prioritize one over the other.

Turn the Other Cheek?

Beyond abusive relationships, this chapter also raises a broader question. How can we guarantee that when we deal with people, we care for ourselves and protect the relationship? That must be an overriding question every time we deal with others – in good and bad relationships. To be sure we can protect ourselves and our dignity, we must always watch how we are caring for ourselves. Self-care, or watching out for our own well-being, goes beyond taking a regular bath, brushing our teeth, or eating properly. It also involves protecting yourself from harm – including emotional harm, which can come from relating with others.

Unfortunately, sometimes in our desire to be peacemakers, we as Christians can sacrifice our own well-being. I mentioned that our guiding Scripture for this book is by Paul:

> Do all that you can to live in peace with everyone. Dear friends, never take revenge. Leave that to the righteous anger of God. For the Scriptures say, "I will take revenge; I will pay them back," says the Lord. Instead, "If your enemies are hungry, feed him. If they are thirsty, give them something to drink. In doing this, you will heap burning coals on their heads." Don't let evil conquer you, but conquer evil by doing good. (Romans 12:18-21)

However, it is essential to qualify what the Bible means by this and other teachings for peace. Unfortunately, these Scriptures have been taken out of context and misused, leading to abuse and taking advantage of many people. Yes, we are called to be peacemakers and to live in peace, but that should not be understood that we are doormats or, worse, willing victims for anyone abusing or injuring us. We must add that there is nothing in these verses or other teachings in the Bible that offer a blanket teaching to acquiesce blindly and carelessly to guarantee peace. We can and should work to secure a peace not based on abuse.

No single teaching about peacemaking has been more misunderstood and misapplied than Jesus's teaching about turning the other cheek. Here is Jesus's teaching in context:

"You have heard that the law that says the punishment must match the injury: 'An eye for an eye, and a tooth for a tooth.' But I say, do not resist an evil person! If someone slaps you on the right cheek, offer the other cheek also. If you are sued in court and your shirt is taken from you, give your coat too." (Matthew 5:38-40)

What teachings have you heard that originate with these verses? I have heard things like, "Christians should submit to whatever" – even to abuse and injustice. People may also advocate for being meek, since the meek shall inherit the earth, according to Matthew 5:5. The NLT, however, uses the word *humble*. When people claim Christians should be tame and submit even to abuse, they misinterpret the Bible.

First, we need to look at the Scripture Jesus was quoting. "An eye for an eye, and a tooth for a tooth" comes from the Old Testament justice system. Leviticus 24:17-20 says:

Anyone who takes another person's life must be put to death. Anyone who kills another person's animal must pay for it in full – a live animal for the animal that was killed. Anyone who injures another person must be dealt with according to the injury inflicted – a fracture for a fracture, an eye for an eye, a tooth for a tooth. Whatever anyone does to injure another person must be paid back in kind.

The purpose of the law was that the punishment fit the crime and did not escalate into revenge. The principle was also applied elsewhere in the law. For instance, if you were irresponsible with someone's property, you were required to compensate the victim, but limits were set on what was fair compensation. The goal was to protect and restore everyone's property, while maintaining relationships (Exodus 22:10-15).

This form of retribution makes sense in that case. However, some forms of retribution are difficult to envisage and are primarily offered as deterrents for carelessness and abuse. For example, if the courts gouge out your eye because you made me blind, you would have received equal punishment/revenge, but this form of retribution is not always productive.

That is why Jesus suggests a different way to respond. Martin Luther King, Jr., an ordained minister and prominent civil-rights leader, observed in 1958,

> Violence as a way of achieving racial justice is both impractical and immoral. It is impractical because it is a descending spiral ending in destruction for all. The old law of an eye for an eye leaves everybody blind. It is immoral because it seeks to humiliate the opponent rather than win his understanding; it seeks to annihilate rather than to convert.[6]

King is saying here that the principle of the law – to not escalate violence through punishment – should be taken further. He based this on Jesus's teachings of loving others as we love ourselves and not seeking revenge to settle accounts. For King, the practical results of that exercise would be the destruction of society and not an actual achievement of justice.

Non-violence to Raise Consciousness

Jesus teaches us not to ignore injustice but to hold the perpetrator accountable in a way that restores rather than destroys them and society. Imagine a situation where, if someone forced you to give up your coat or dress, you also gave them your vest or underwear. This

---

6   Martin Luther King, Jr., *Stride Toward Freedom: The Montgomery Story* (Boston: Beacon Press, 1958), 208.

would be considered demeaning and excessive in any culture, especially in shame-based cultures. It is a public shaming of the highest order. By taking their initial exploitative request further – to the point that you are shamefully exposed – you would also be shaming them for their lack of concern about human dignity. So, when Jesus tells people to turn the other cheek, he is not teaching blind compliance, but rather a reasoned approach that would engage the perpetrator in their sin, without the victim becoming sucked into being a perpetrator themselves.

Notice that Jesus does not tell the victim to run away (take flight) or fight back. Instead, the victim may meet the perpetrator's demands but also do even more. Going further, it is as if the victim is telling the perpetrator, "Do you see what you are doing? You are abusing your power and position." The victim demands a reason for the person's act and shows the perpetrator he or she is wrong. We should not condone sin and abuse, nor sweep injury under the carpet. We must be willing to stand up against it by lovingly confronting the perpetrator with their sin.

How can we be sure that is what Jesus means? Fortunately, we have a record of both Jesus and Paul actually being struck on the cheek and how they responded. Jesus demanded a reason for the perpetrator's action by asking the high priest's officer why he struck him (John 18). Paul does a similar thing when, before the Sanhedrin, the priest hits him (Acts 23:1-3). He calls out the priest's sin and questions the Council's judgements. Hence Jesus is not saying we should just stand by and let people do whatever they want. We need to confront the evil done, but without reacting in a way that adds to the evil already being done. Sometimes you need to accept a significant cost (unfairly), move on, and forgive. Jesus is teaching us to be agents of peace and non-retaliation. Paul offers the same teaching by encouraging us to let God apply the revenge rather than ourselves (Romans 12:19).

It is interesting to note that Jesus and Paul were both struck while in court, undergoing a trial by the religious councils of the day. Much abuse can happen when someone in power accuses you of a crime or in corrupt legal contexts. It is like modern-day police violence, which is prevalent in many countries. It might be helpful to learn the proper reaction processes in your context when this is likely to happen, since, as we discussed already, your safety is important.

An unconventional example of raising a corrupt perpetrator's consciousness about their part in injustice was the women's protests in Kenya in the early 1990s, led by the mothers of detained political prisoners. These women staged a sit-in and hunger strike at what they called Freedom Corner in a busy public park, demanding the release of their sons and a stop to the detentions.

After several warnings by the government, a heavily armed contingent of riot police was sent in to disperse and arrest the women. The mothers dropped their clothes and bared their bodies publicly and in front of the media to protest the shame (or shamelessness) of the battalion of young men (of around their sons' ages) and, by extension, the government. Culturally, if a son saw his mother naked, it was a curse against his life.

Public response was swift, resulting in more people joining the protests or condemning the government nationally and internationally. As a result, the government relented, ceasing their assaults against the women. Although it took some time to release all their sons from prison, the shaming from the stripping incident marked a turning point. Justice was eventually done by stopping a corrupt act. Of course, public stripping and cursing people specifically aren't generally considered proper courses of action in resolving conflicts. However, using these extreme non-violent approaches has its place in dealing with injustices in unique circumstances such as these.

We must also remember that Jesus took a very firm stand against injustice, especially against the vulnerable. On the day he began his public ministry, he quoted Isaiah and said he had fulfilled the Scripture:

> "The Spirit of the Lord is upon me, for he has anointed me to bring Good News to the poor. He has sent me to proclaim that captives will be released, that the blind will see, that the oppressed will be set free, and that the tome of the Lord's favour has come" (Luke 4:18-19).

Christ came as a fulfilment to all the teachings of the prophets, such as Isaiah, who castigates the rich and powerful who take advantage of the poor and weak, declaring that God will destroy them (Isaiah 5:8), or Jeremiah, who calls on the people to "be fair-minded and just. Do what is right! Help those who have been robbed; rescue them from their oppressors. Give up your evil deeds! Do not mistreat foreigners, orphans, and widows. Stop murdering the innocent!" (Jeremiah 22:3). This call to do justice and defend the weak is echoed by almost all the prophets of the Old Testament (see Isaiah 56:1; Hosea 12:6; Amos 5:24; Zechariah 7:9). With whatever power you have, Jesus and the prophets say, you should stand up for the oppressed, defend the weak, and pursue justice.

Although we are called peacemakers, this does not mean we accommodate abuse in the name of false peace. All abuse is evil and there is no room for it in human relationships. A person who has sold themselves out to corruption can occasion significant conflict. Evil acts like sexual abuse, child or spousal mistreatment and discrimination, for example, are wrong and even punishable under the law. The Bible warns against such by admonishing, "Take no part in the worthless deeds of evil and darkness; instead, expose them. It is shameful even to talk about the things that ungodly people do in secret" (Ephesians 5:11-12). In this situation, there is no room for negotiation. We should have nothing to do with them but expose them.

Conclusion

What should our friend Ojai do? We know that he took advantage of others, abusing his power when in government. But he is now also a victim of the pastor's blackmail, which can be seen as a symptom of abuse. Ojai is trapped. The manipulative pastor has undue power over him and can use Ojai's vulnerability and past misdeeds to control him. Should he defy the pastor? What if the pastor reports his misdeeds, and the case is re-opened? What is the cost of giving in to the pastor's demands? Should Ojai turn the other cheek and continue in this abusive web he is caught in? I doubt that Jesus would tell him that that is the best solution. It might help him to own up to his reality and risk the fallout by breaking free from this controlling relationship.

In this chapter, we discussed how abuse works to control someone when victims have no means to defend themselves. If possible, anyone facing abuse should seek help, and remove themselves from the situation. In other situations, where one's well-being is at stake, be careful about applying the advice to "turn the other cheek". Turning the other cheek is, in fact, not a call to simply subject oneself to abuse, but to raise the perpetrator's consciousness through non-violent confrontation.

You are planning to meet up with a friend who has confided in you that they are dealing with abuse within a relationship. What are some things you could say to validate the person or encourage them for being vulnerable enough to share? How could you reassure them that abuse was not their fault and help them consider options to get help?

....

....

....

....

....

....

....

....

Group Discussion

1. Read Romans 12:18-21 and Matthew 5:38-40. Discuss what you believe these Scriptures teach about conflict transformation. Give examples of instances in which you have heard either or both Scriptures taught incorrectly. How can you help correct these false teachings?

2. What protections are there in place in your society to help those facing abuse? Are those enough? What needs to change?

11

Celebrate Success

> *Nyama 'nke yaria bokima 'kee* (KISII, KENYA).
> "A small piece of meat can help consume large quantity of ugali."
> **MEANING:** Do not underestimate the potential of a small effort.

For as long as Kame can remember, her large family gathered at the homes of various aunties and uncles for parties and hangouts. It helped that their families were all settled in the same location. Kame grew up in the company of over 20 cousins. At some point, she did not even know who her brothers and sisters were because they were in and out of each other's homes so regularly. Any child was welcome at any time of the day or night.

When Kame was about 19 years old, the family went through a crisis. Kame and most of the cousins were unsure what the real issues were, but they noticed that the families stopped meeting for the usual parties and get-togethers. There also seemed to be a growing animosity between their families.

"This is insane. None of my cousins are returning my texts or calls. Why can't I connect with my cousins any more?" Kame lamented to her mother. "What's caused this break-up anyway?"

"I don't know the details either," said Kame's mom in a sad voice. "People have withdrawn from our family just like that. No one is talking to your dad or me any more. Do you think it is because your dad and I just purchased a new farm in another district and are looking to move there?"

"What does that have to do with anything? That's our family's choice, and we can live wherever we want," Kame retorted.

"Sometimes you just can't understand the animosity with some people, even within the family. There is great jealousy in seeing our progress. Not everyone in the family is excited about that. You may not know that Uncle Jairo and others even tried to sabotage the purchase. They spread some terrible rumours about us stealing the money we are using to buy the farm. So sad, because your dad and I have been sacrificing and saving this money for over 10 years. Do they want us all to just stay here and be miserable? But we are not going to be held back by mean people. Your father and I made the right decision, whether they like it or not. We are moving and never coming back. Who do they think they are?"

A few days after, Kame went to visit Uncle Jairo. She had been close to his daughter, her cousin, so she had often been at his house. "Uncle Jairo, I have been wondering why there seems to be a break in our family's communication. We haven't had our usual parties for a whole year. And most of my cousins stopped talking to me. Do you have an idea why?"

"Kame," Uncle Jairo replied in a subdued tone, "this is a matter for the elders in the family to address. Nothing for you to worry about."

"But I am worried. We have lost all our cherished family ties. Mum tells me it is because Dad bought a farm across the district, and some of you are unhappy?"

"It is not the farm or how far it is. If you must know, your dad did not care to consult the rest of us. We are family, Kame, and we share all things. Why would he just go off by himself and do this? Isn't keeping our family together important to him?"

"But, Uncle, Dad is only trying to provide for us, his family. We are moving, but the new place is only two hours away. We can still visit each other."

"Maybe, maybe, my daughter," Jairo responded.

"Would you help me heal this break, Uncle Jairo?" Kame asked. "I believe that you, as the eldest in our clan, have a responsibility to help."

Uncle Jairo did not say anything.

"And what is more important? That my dad consult with you or that he try something that you have all been teaching us, the kids: to be bold and explore life beyond this village?" Kame asked.

"Look here, Kame," Uncle Jairo interjected. "Sure, my brother has always been bold. But boldness can be the mark of a fool! Your parents are a stubborn bunch. They do not listen to me or anyone else. Why did they send you to me now? Why are they not the ones talking to me? You see, this is what I am saying – stubborn people!" Jairo's voice was rising.

"But, Uncle, why must we split up the family like this?"

"Don't ask me. Ask your parents," he said, walking away.

Learning from Our Cultures

This book advocates for preserving relationships and as much as possible, cooperating in settling disputes, which is more likely to lead to better understanding and peace. Traditional African methods may have something to teach us in this process, especially in how we celebrate our newfound transformation after a settlement. Indeed, the celebration, both at the interpersonal and community levels, helps to ground the positive change in a way that reminds us of the power of peaceful coexistence.

As Kame's story reminds us, traditionally, many communities practised forms of celebration that marked the end of conflict and animosity. Among the Meru people of Kenya, disputes were brought before village elders whenever the parties could not address them themselves. If this were successful, the elders would offer their determination and help the parties settle the dispute. If this did not work, the parties would be encouraged to go to the Njuri Ncheke, the supreme governing council, for arbitration. This judicial body was instrumental in helping maintain harmony within the tribe by adjudicating the most severe crimes and settling land disputes, including grazing sites, saltlicks, forests, and agricultural allotments.

The Njuri Ncheke was also known for celebrating whenever a case was determined through them. Since there were no court fees, as there are in modern judicial systems, the parties were required to offer bulls, goats, or lambs to the council. These were slaughtered and consumed together in a ceremony with the council members, the disputants, and other members of the community – including family and friends of the disputants. This ritual also invocated the ancestors and the divine as witnesses to the settlement. The tribal priests, who were part of the Njuri Ncheke, officiated at these celebration ceremonies. To make these meaningful, the council would set a date, and many of the disputants would congregate and take part in the ceremonies, which included eating and being merry together, as a sign of accepting the settlement. The community was also welcome as witnesses to the settlement.

Similar processes can be found in many African tribes and communities. Traditional customary law practices were designed to settle disputes and bring harmony to the community and effect justice. Although these were varied in their structural composition, they followed a similar arrangement as that of the Meru, with elders' councils at different levels making decisions. The results were primarily win-win, with a strong expectation for reconciliation and maintaining peace at individual and communal levels.

Of course, the rise of independent federal states and law systems across the continent in the last 70 years has also come with centralized legal and judicial court systems. While some hybrid systems recognize mediation and other alternative dispute-resolution processes, for the most part, these new forms of justice are competitive and uncooperative. They are patterned after Western justice and legal systems, most of which are litigious and overly competitive. These win-lose practices frame conflict in terms of achieving an outcome for one party instead of restoring a relationship.

Celebrate the Restored Relationship

Celebrating together acknowledges the importance and value of the relationship. It affirms that peace is essential to sustain this valuable bond. We see this in the parable of the prodigal son (Luke 15:11-32). Jesus narrated a story that resonated with the Jewish people of his time and applies to many African contexts. The younger son's decision to leave home and claim his inheritance before the father's death was incredibly disruptive. Indeed, in the Near East (and most African cultures), the father's inheritance was only given after the father passed away, and even then, not right away – it often took several years to acquire what the father owned. No one in their right mind would have rushed to inherit from their father, and never would that happen when he was alive. The son's demand to have his inheritance from his father effectively meant that he was "wishing him dead." This appalling demand was considered an offence as serious as murdering his father. The result was conflict at an unthinkable level.

The wayward son subsequently took off to a far county and squandered his share of the inheritance in careless living. Later, when he came to his senses and finally returned home, his father, in an incalculably priceless sign of love and forgiveness, threw a party to celebrate his son's return. He not only forgave him but brought him back home with honour: "Quick! Bring the finest robe in the house and put it on him. Get a ring for his finger and sandals for his feet. And kill the calf we have been fattening. We must celebrate with a feast" (Luke 15:22-23). The father was thankful for a restored son and a healed relationship. In trying to win over his other son, the father remarked, "We had to celebrate this happy day. For your brother was dead and has come back to life! He was lost, but now he is found!" (Luke 15:32). This restored relationship called for a celebration. The family was back together, and there was a cause to rejoice.

Of course, Jesus was teaching about the mercy of God towards his wayward sons and daughters. Indeed, earlier in this same chapter, Jesus had shared that heaven rejoices when one sinner repents (Luke 15:7). This is the ultimate restored relationship: for a sinner to repent and be converted into a relationship with God. But Jesus might have also been giving us a hint on how to live out the restoration of our relationships mediated by repentance and forgiveness. We, too, should rejoice in the beauty of our restored relationships, especially if the original break caused us pain.

The father's choice to celebrate was costly but showed what he values most. The father's shockingly joyful reception showed he cared little for his wealth and his honour and cared deeply about his relationships with his sons. If it cost him his legacy and his fatted calf, that was nothing compared to the value he placed on reconciliation. We see the priority of reconciliation in how the father mourned his son and even kept watch until he returned. He thus took the initiative to love and restore his son, even before the son was back home. He did the same with the older son, who was also sinful because he loved his father's wealth rather than his father for the man he was. The father loved them both and, in restoring both to a relationship with him and with each other, ordered celebrations.

Like the father's party, celebration can be a way to boldly acknowledge yours and others' brokenness but also to highlight the potential for human relationships. In that way, festivities proclaim the power of redemptive love. Consider Jesus's last supper with his 12 disciples (John 13). Jesus eats this important meal with his closest friends whom he has done everything with for the past three years. In a few hours, one will betray him, another will deny him, and all the disciples will run away to cower at his arrest.

By having a meal with these disciples, Jesus inaugurates a practice Christians carry out today to celebrate God's invitation to a relationship with all of us, even we who, through our sinful nature, hate him. It is also a call for us to invite others into relationships – even people who might betray or hurt us.

At the beginning of this book, I talked about how costly conflict can be, a fire that can destroy if it is not controlled. Celebration helps us remember the conflict's cost and may deter us from falling into the same rut. The prodigal son could not imagine insulting his father again after that party. The Lord's Supper reminds us of Jesus's sacrifice so that we take our sin seriously. Conflicts and their transformation help us recognise just how costly a break is. It challenges us to imagine a different relationship and, if we are wise, encourages us to seek peace with all and not to let issues pile up, because the alternative is very costly.

At the same time, the celebration itself can be costly. The father's generosity towards the son was indeed costly; the party was expensive. The slaughtered animal in the Njuri Ncheke celebration was costly, a lost life. But these demonstrate that the cost of reconciliation is worthwhile and less costly than a broken relationship.

Celebrate to Encourage Peace

Conflicts can feel daunting, even overwhelming, especially when they are emotional and drawn out. Many of us, even when we resolve a conflict situation, are worn out, and may want to rest or take a break. What you feel is the effect of conflict that, like a fire, burns or purifies but rarely leaves us the same. Fire transforms our relationship with the other, for good or for worse.

Of course, in a committed relationship like marriage or working in a team, it is not like you can easily take a break or walk away. You must stay engaged in rebuilding the relationship. To counter the tiredness and negativity conflict can leave, take time to celebrate when a conflict has been resolved. The celebration process does not have to be elaborate. However, it is essential to move beyond resolving the conflict to the real results: enjoying a better relationship.

Celebration is worth the investment because it forms a habit of peacebuilding. When we celebrate, our brains register that this thing we are celebrating is something good and worth emphasizing. By rewarding these behaviours, we develop positive associations with conflict resolution. If we do this often, we prioritize peace and invest further in it. Similarly, we value what we spend time thinking about and investing in. When we spend time nurturing our relationships, whether through conflict transformation or otherwise, we value them further and so invest in them, allowing them to flourish.

Another reason to celebrate is that it becomes a testimony to others about the potential for conflict transformation. Our ability to agree and restore would-be broken relationships is a gift. Unlike animals that might fight with the intention of harming the other

– even to the death – we can talk things over and agree. Unfortunately, given the many conflicts and broken relationships around the world, we need more examples of the possibilities for agreement and the transformations that this can bring. Indeed, many would be encouraged to hear of a mended relationship, a reversed divorce, forgiveness, and many other restorative processes. Living out your change or sharing your story might encourage others to seek similar opportunities to agree. And what a blessing that would be to spread the optimism of restoring relationships!

How to Celebrate

So, how do you celebrate a transformation in your relationship after a dispute has been addressed? The answer is simply: in any way that makes sense to you and the other party. In other words, there are no hard-and-fast rules for how to do this, just what works for you; but be sure to mark the success in some way that befits the win.

Whenever possible, I encourage whoever is involved in a conflict-restoration process to find ways to celebrate their agreement. Of course, this is impossible if the deal is a cessation of the relationship. But in situations where the agreement is to rebuild, there are good reasons to celebrate. A celebration here does not mean a party, although that will always be welcome if you choose to do that. It can be as small as reviewing the process to commend each other for their willingness to transform the relationship. Or a handshake or a hug that communicates agreement. Whatever you choose, it is crucial to be sure it befits the positive position of your relationship.

Any celebration must be agreed upon by the parties involved. It must never be contrived or forced but rather be a genuine way for the parties to embrace achieving their goals in meaningful ways. Nothing is more disingenuous than a rushed and untruthful agreement and celebration – or one party using the occasion to score points, or gain mileage and power, for instance. This would make the other party feel used or taken advantage of rather than an integral part of the resolution – which, in turn, may mean that agreement will not last in the long term nor be effective in sustaining the relationship. It may also damage trust and destroy the goodwill necessary to address future issues together.

Different circumstances will call for varying levels of celebration. A couple's agreement on a personal dispute may be marked by a smile or a pat on the shoulder as an acknowledgement that the two are past the issue. However, an inter-community conflict may require a public statement and maybe an agreement-signing ceremony.

Even on the international stage, peace agreements and cessations of conflict are often celebrated by sharing gifts, exchanging signed agreements, a handshake, or even a meal. For instance, the Israeli leader Yitzhak Rabin and Yasser Arafat, leader of the Palestine Liberation Organization, signed an agreement superintended by US President Bill Clinton. A historical handshake at the US White House ceremony marked the moment of celebration.

Whatever the scale of the celebration, its significance remains the same. Just as when we celebrate a birthday or graduation, a celebration marks a milestone, big or small, but one that is important in the ongoing transformation of that relationship.

There are several ways to celebrate a conflict resolution, depending on the situation and the people involved. Some options include:

- Holding a celebration or party to mark the resolution and bring people together.
- Recognizing the efforts of individuals or teams who helped resolve the conflict.
- Taking a symbolic action to signify the end of the conflict, such as a handshake, a hug, or a community event like planting a tree or appearing together at a public event.

- Reflecting on the lessons learned from the conflict and how they can be applied in the future.
- Communicating the resolution to all parties involved and seeking feedback and input.
- Reviewing the process of resolving the conflict and making improvements in the event of future conflicts.
- Taking time to relax and celebrate with family and friends.

Of course, celebration does not prevent people from bringing up the issue again if the parties fail to live up to their agreement. In most mediation processes, the parties are encouraged to register their agreement – with the mediator's help. This can be a formal document admissible in court or just points of understanding agreed upon by the parties. In informal settings and interpersonal agreements, these can be verbal agreements the parties promise to keep. Either way, an agreement is necessary, in whatever form, because the parties can refer to it as a touchstone for their renewed commitment to the relationship or the reason for walking away.

Sometimes, it may be important to revisit the agreement at a future date. This is a critical part of the celebration, to have a check-in to review the agreement and recalibrate where necessary.

Brainstorm a few more appropriate ways to celebrate resolved conflicts in your family, workplace, or church.

It is also a great way to honour your efforts and ensure that the resolution holds.

A future check-in point is often required as part of the process of formal mediation. The mediator sets a time to meet with the parties again to review what is working or not working when it comes to their agreement. This step provides the opportunity to make sure the deal is the right one and that the parties still see the resolutions as reasonable. This is a time to affirm the parties regarding their relationship and support their growth.

When and How *Not* to Celebrate

Are there situations where celebrations are out of the question? The short answer is YES. Sometimes, an agreement is impossible, or whatever you agree on is just not enough. When the relationship has been terminated, or one party is unwilling to reconcile, it is hard to celebrate the relationship. There is no need to seek further contact or assess how the deals worked or did not work. My failed grant contract is one example, as is someone rescued from an abusive relationship. That person does not need to engage with the abuser any more, but may celebrate the rescue in a manner most appropriate to her or him.

Where the disagreement is mutual, and the two parties cannot strike a balance or agree on a way forward, the agreement might be to separate, transforming the relationship in a way that does not require further contact. Or one or both parties may agree that the decisions reached are sufficient and do not want to revisit the issues. Either way, a celebration is best chosen by the parties in conflict.

Is it appropriate to celebrate a relationship that has ended? I believe that, in the case of escaping abuse, yes. A celebration of some kind may help you recast your circumstances mentally as a positive outcome. It may also be necessary to grieve the loss of a relationship.

How you do that is dependent on your situation. It might be a simple matter of seeking professional or other help in order to move on from the situation. It might also be a mental process of putting the abuse in its place, accepting that you were not responsible for the pain you endured, and that you are not to blame for it.

Another perspective to consider is how not to celebrate. You may be excited about the outcome, but there are better ways to show that than bragging about winning. Pride serves very little to support the long-term growth of a relationship, and making the other party look like a fool or having lost will be interpreted in bad faith. Celebrate in a way that does not offend others or cast them in a bad light, but instead honours the dignity of the other and encourages goodwill toward future engagements.

Beyond Ourselves

I saw the power of celebration when I consulted for an NGO. Conflicts among employees were sabotaging the accomplishment of the organisation's mission, and some employees had left. In their exit interviews, they voiced their displeasure at the organisation's toxicity levels.

In interviews with me, current and former employees felt that one cause of the toxic culture was the lack of clearly defined goals for the organization and unclear communication lines between departments and individuals. In my interviews with the senior leadership, even the overall goals of the NGO did not seem sufficiently explicit. This seeped deep into the departments and individual workers. New employees had to muddle through to establish what they were supposed to be doing, whom they needed to collaborate with, and what results were to be expected.

We conducted an organization-wide survey with the senior leadership to identify training needs. We developed a new employee training process to highlight the vision and mission of the organization and expected behaviour once hired. The leadership and the employees defined life-giving values they would like to see embodied in the organization. We developed a renewed vision/mission statement based on care for the employees and one another. The CEO invited me to re-train all the employees on the new expectations, beginning with the senior leadership. Although some individuals chose not to buy in to the new processes, most people were eager because they were tired of having to deal with the poor functioning of the organization.

I go into all this detail to show that the process was a lot of work – and took two years. Afterward, we organized a "graduation party" to celebrate. The leadership printed certificates of completion for all staff members who completed the training, signed by the CEO, me, and the board chair. The certificates acknowledged each employee's commitment to the organization and the renewed values of collaboration, positivity, and action.

> **Highlight an experience of celebrating a resolved conflict and restored relationship that you witnessed. What made this experience memorable?**
>
> ....
>
> ....
>
> ....
>
> ....
>
> ....
>
> ....
>
> ....

I have been in touch with the leadership of this NGO for years, and they report better internal relations and a more explicit mission and values. The administration holds an annual celebration party where they recognize good performance and give awards for positivity, best attitude at work, and collaboration. Fewer employees have left the organization, and the results of their work have improved tremendously. This story shows the impact of crafting a collaborative solution, focusing on relationships, and celebrating success.

If you would like to share your story of a transformed conflict as a testament to growing relationships, please go to my website **www.mediatepeace.com**. You are welcome to read exciting stories from others too!

Conclusion

Kame was broken. She knew this split would only heal if Uncle Jairo was involved. But she remembered that she could always approach other elders in the village, and so that is what she did. After several attempts, the headman and several elders of the village got some of the uncles and their families together for a meeting at Kame's home.

"Good people of Mwano's family," the headman called, "your family has been one of the examples of unbreakable solidarity in this village. We are, therefore, saddened by the enmity that seems to be breaking you apart the past few years. We don't have a solution for this ourselves, but we have brought all of us together to figure out how we can help."

Other elders joined in, begging the family members to reconsider their conflict. After several hours of talking, there was finally a breakthrough.

"I want to apologize for my lack of solidarity with my family," Kame's dad confessed. "I thought I should do whatever I wanted by myself. But now I see that the blessings of the rest of the family, and indeed my community, are necessary. I ask for forgiveness and invite your blessings on our move."

"What shall we say, people of Mwano?" The headman looked at Jairo as the representative of the family.

"I see your point," Jairo said, looking at his brother. "And congratulations on your courage. You are cutting a new path for our family, across the ranges. We should be proud of that. We all got carried away by this. But I see that that is not good. Tell you what, I will call a meeting . . . no, I want a party at my home next month. Let's celebrate your new venture. We might even ask the *Padri* (pastor) to join us and bless you all as you prepare to move."

"That would be a great thing, Jairo. I knew I could count on you. You are a good man! Thank you," the headman said, extending his hand to Jairo. "We are happy to join the family in celebration, and to bless Kame's family on this move. Let us know when we can be back for the feast!" the headman concluded with joy.

It is never easy to mend a strained relationship, move past old grievances, or restore broken trust. It takes empathy, communication, and patience. It is a process of learning more about ourselves and one another. When we accomplish something so significant, it is a cause for great joy! We are marking the tenacity of the human spirit, the value of collaboration, and the power of forgiveness. We renew our bonds and express gratitude for each other's reconciliation efforts. It allows us to evaluate our past accomplishments, show gratitude for the here and now, and envision a more promising future together. That is worth celebrating!

Share your story at **www.mediatepeace.com**

Think of someone who you have resolved a conflict with recently. Write a note affirming how much you value them and the restored relationship and consider sending it to them.

....

....

....

....

....

....

....

....

Group Discussion

1. Earlier in this book, we talked about how conflict originated with Adam and Eve and God's efforts to reconcile the relationship. Jesus's story of the prodigal son points us to what happens after our relationship with the Father God is restored: an eternal celebration! If eternity is a celebration of a resolved conflict, how does that influence the way you want to relate with God?

2. How does that influence the way you want to relate with people?

12

Growth after Fire

> **Izendla ziyagezans** (Zulu, South Africa).
> "Hands wash each other."
> **Meaning:** We are on this earth to help each other and build each other up. No one exists in a vacuum.

An NGO based in the US stopped sending programme funds to their partner in Uganda, stating that the Ugandan partner was not properly accounting for and reporting how funds were being used. The Uganda partner threatened to cut links and move on with other funders. They cut off communications and stopped responding to the US office. The two were in a stalemate.

I was travelling to Uganda, so the US director asked that I meet with the CEO of the Uganda team to help understand their issues. The Ugandan CEO felt the US partner was approaching him and his team as "kids", making unreasonable demands, threatening to stop the funding and even to sue them. He and the Uganda team had decided to stop communicating to "teach the Americans a lesson": the lesson that they could manage without US funds. They wanted to be treated as equal partners and to negotiate the demands for stringent accountability. If the US team continued to treat them with suspicion, they were ready to forego the funds and had already made progress in seeking new support from Europe and Australia.

I raised the funder's need to be sure that the funds were being used as specified for the agreed programmes and following the proper time frames. The Ugandan director argued that he understood this, but the needs they sometimes confronted could not be accomplished with the funds provided and according to the schedules set. This was frustrating for him and his team. Additionally, the reporting processes were unfamiliar and sometimes challenging for them. Working through contractors and in rural communities meant reports took longer, so they couldn't fill in the reports as quickly as their US colleagues expected, but that did not mean they were stealing the funds.

After about two hours of conversation, I could see why the misunderstanding had arisen. Both sides had genuine demands, but communication had broken down between them over their differing expectations and needs. I was able to report back to the US partner and facilitate a video meeting between the two groups. After six monthly meetings, an improved finance reporting process was smoothed out, and the organizations were working together again.

A relationship was saved. Dignity and respect were affirmed. Donors continued to bless people. Most importantly, the needy people served in Uganda continued to benefit from the great work the partners were doing together.

As Iron Sharpens Iron

As the international partners realized – and this book has emphasized – we are created for relationships, not going it alone. We need to stick together in order to encourage one another as we face difficulties

(Hebrews 10:27). But being with others also means that we should expect difficulties like conflicts.

Dealing with other people can cause friction. An affront or challenge to how we have done things or our perspectives is never easy. It is a challenge to change; because we are creatures of habit, change can sometimes feel like an attack on who we are. Like the NGO partners, we are tempted to react negatively, because the demands are often uncomfortable.

But friction with others can be valuable in our process of change and growth. The book of Proverbs says, "As iron sharpens iron, so a friend sharpens a friend" (Proverbs 27:17). Sharpening a knife involves friction and being ground down; the knife is not left the same. Without sharpening, the tool is dull and ineffective. Cutting through a piece of meat takes half as much effort with a sharp knife.

Other people, like iron, grind our dullness away, helping us to be sharper – often through conflict. We become wiser, and even more competent in handling life's issues. I don't mean that we should seek out conflicts so that we can "sharpen" ourselves or others. Don't worry – that grinding down will come when we interact with another person! But, when it does, we learn to treasure these conflict experiences because they offer useful results.

Recall a conflict you have had in your life. In what ways did that conflict help you change and grow to become a better person?

. . . .

. . . .

. . . .

. . . .

A few years ago, my teenage son often did the opposite of what I advised, simply because he wanted to be independent. He was also quick to blame me when things did not turn out his way. I felt he was disrespecting me by not adopting my suggestions. But I was even more frustrated because, as he was moving out of the home, I knew he needed my help and guidance to prepare for that.

After about a year, I recognized my role in developing the relationship and decided to change this reality. I initiated lunch dates and attended sports events just so that the two of us could talk about us. It was awkward at first, but he eventually began to warm up and even apologized. I apologized for my reaction too. We agreed that he would seek advice if needed and that I would expect him to take only some of my advice. This helped us re-establish our relationship. Almost seven years after, our relationship has only gotten better.

Understanding is thus indeed possible if we are willing to have our iron edges shaved off a bit in our sharpening. Sometimes it takes humility, like in my relationship with my son. Other times, it takes intervention by an objective party, like in the case of the US and Ugandan organizations. Either way, addressing disagreements has the potential to bring us better relationships. Relationships do not just grow by themselves. We need to put in the time and effort to weed, water, and invest in their growth.

Rising from the Ashes

Of course, sometimes, even when you have done all you could, the fire might get out of control, rage on, and burn you or your bridges. The result is ashes, instead of a baked cake.

Sometimes, there is still hope that the burned-out relationship can be resurrected. And yet I recognize the sad reality that you can do all this book advocates, learn about yourself, act to address the hurts, and still have a relationship end. The raging fires of conflict burned all attempts at reconciliation and the hopes of restoring the relationship, sometimes for good.

Ending up in an ash pit is disappointing for anyone. It can feel like a failure. I have never met any divorced person who does not wish they could restore what they had at the beginning of their life with their spouse. Neither do business people dragging each other through courts celebrate that process.

This destruction can leave a sense of failure or regret for what you invested – or wished you had invested – in the relationship. There is nothing much you can do to escape this trauma. Instead, you may need to accept the reality and seek to learn, heal, and move on.

Still, you may be able to find some gems in the rough of conflict – in fact, conflicts are some of the best laboratories for growth. Indeed, if reviewed with this growth mindset, you may be surprised by what you have learned from the experience.

Do you remember my story about a friend who took me for a ride and used my expertise to land a big grant only to cut me off? I took some time to review this experience. Over the years, I have managed to perfect my engagement with other people – friends or not – when it comes to employing my expertise. I am happy to support anyone using my knowledge. But if that support will be for pay, I have developed agreements we must sign before any engagement. This has served me and those I work with well. I would never have achieved this professionalization of my help if I had not gone through that painful experience with my friend.

Of course, you do not need to go through a conflict to learn. But if you do, please take the time to review the process carefully. It may surprise you that the dish you burned as you were trying to cook it was not in vain. You have developed skills that will benefit you greatly in the future. If this is all conflict offers us, it is still helpful.

Finding Support

Sometimes, transforming a conflict, rebuilding a relationship, or growing after the end of a relationship feels impossible on your own. In an intractable conflict, reach out for resources that can help you break the log jam.

Counselling or therapy are particularly important tools for personal and group growth. The counselor or therapist is trained to understand the social and relationship needs we all face. As I have dealt with different issues in my marriage and workplace, I have greatly benefitted from counselling. You can also consider counselling and therapy when you fail to gain traction and the relationship fails. Sometimes unofficial counsellors can also fill this need, either because they are experienced or because of the confidence placed in them by the community. I highly recommend locating a counsellor or therapist in your community and using their skills.

Many churches and other worship communities have counsellors to support their communities or teach relational skills. I have been a beneficiary, and now teach some of these skills, including individual conflict management, listening, anger management, and group dynamics. Please take advantage of any of these courses wherever you can find them. They are invaluable.

> **Do a quick internet search or ask people you know for contacts of counsellors, therapists, or mediators in your community. Write their contact details below to consult when needed.**
>
> ....
>
> ....
>
> ....
>
> ....

While counsellors and therapists may mostly work with you as an individual or a group for growth, a mediator is a better go-between for individuals or groups in conflict. Mediators are crucial resources for working through issues with others. They may be formally or sometimes informally trained. Their role is to assist parties in addressing and resolving the disagreements. They may be appointed by a court or through a private agreement between the conflicting parties. Depending on the country or jurisdiction, when appointed by a court of law, the decision between the parties in the presence of the mediator is a binding and enforceable legal agreement.

More countries use mediators' expertise to ease the strain on the court systems. Mediation is one part of Alternative Dispute Resolution (ADR) programmes. These programmes are growing in number worldwide and with marked success in their effectiveness. For example, many studies also show that mediation is cheaper, achieves better results in resolving issues, and has a better chance of restoring relationships.

Seek out trainings and resources to grow your conflict competency, especially those that are affordable and locally accessible in your community. There are many helpful international organizations as well. I have been volunteering with the Rotary Peace Fellows for about a decade now. You can look up my website for suggestions of more organizations and resources: **www.mediatepeace.com**. Whatever resource you choose, ensure that it equips you with a broad set of crucial conflict-handling skills you can apply to your relationships now.

Conclusion

Do you remember the scary image of a fire raging across the savannah? Sometimes even these big fires are not as damaging as they first seem. Conservationists believe fires are still a force of good in nature, especially within the animal parks. When these fires burn, the growth that ensues leads to rejuvenated grasslands that are better for the animals. The fires may also help destroy disease pathogens, protecting both the animals and vegetation. All this must be managed, though. Conservationists and park managers do not just set fires carelessly. There is always a plan in place that prevents aimlessly injuring animals or destroying the environment. They do this by controlling the spread of the fires, within a predetermined region, for a specific purpose.

Experiencing a conflict can feel like the savannah grasslands are on fire. Like a fire, conflict can be disruptive. However, when properly harnessed, and in an appropriate and timely manner, it can provide incredible energy toward growth and serve as a needed impetus for change. In this book, I demonstrate that even the most devastating conflicts can lead to new growth. It all depends on whether we let it burn uncontrollably or manage it and guide it towards transformation. Experiencing the benefits of peacebuilding for myself and others energizes and inspires me to build peace. At the end of a conflict, I find there are often better relationships – or at least greater wisdom. As you have read through this book, I hope you have been able to reflect on your experiences, learn about yourself and your relationships, and have already begun to see positive results. Of course, mastery takes practice. You will not become an expert on day one, but committing to applying these principles will help you develop your conflict transformation skills. I wish you freedom from the myths your family may have taught you, your fears about engaging with others in relationships, or the patterns you feel stuck in.

Seeking to live peacefully with others is where you want to be. I hope this book has kindled an ember that you will fan into a different kind of fire by developing your skills to be an astute peacebuilder within your space. I also hope you will train others to do the same.

Wouldn't it be great for all of us to learn how not to be burned by the fires of conflict that ignite in our lives, and instead control these as well-managed fires to help us build our lives? Can you imagine if we all had the remarkable skill to confront others lovingly, listen actively, address issues, and seek peace with all?

Yes, I want to live in a world where my attitudes are judged only after I have engaged with the other fully. I want to lead with a positive approach to others and not assume they always mean evil. I want to learn about others' needs and collaborate to solve the problems between us.

Peace is possible. And it starts with us!

Write down your main takeaways from this book. What steps to transforming conflicts and developing your relationships are you going to take?

....

....

....

....

....

....

Group Discussion

1. What areas of growth did you notice through the study of this book – individual, family, and your community? What steps will you be taking to make that happen?

2. After reading this book, is there something you learned about that you are curious to explore further? Where could you find resources to help you continue to grow?

Engage further in conflict and relationship skills development, access resources, and share your stories at **www.mediatepeace.com**.

Acknowledgements

No one writes a book like this alone, without the input and influence of a close community. That community was my dear wife, Victoria, now in the Lord's presence. You taught me to fight fair and to build a relationship with someone you care deeply about. It is also our two sons, Tim and Wega. You, my family, regularly keep me honest!

My community is also the people I have met in places I have been blessed to call home and the workplaces that sharpen my relationship skills. That includes my current Regis University community with colleagues who often teach me about conflict transformation in our work relationships and my students who teach me new lessons.

Finally, this book would not have come to be without the ministry of Oasis International Publishing and their support. Specifically, Hannah Rasmussen guided the idea generation, writing, countless revisions, and every other step of the process. I owe a ton to you, Hannah!

To God be the glory!
Dr M.D. Kinoti

Oasis will become the first publisher capable of placing a book or Bible in every Christian reader's hand in Africa.
Go to oasisinternationalpublishing.com to learn more.

THE DISCIPLER'S TOOLKIT
George M. Mutuku and Mark A. Olander
The churches in Sub-Saharan Africa are growing numerically, primarily through evangelism. But evangelism is only the beginning of the disciple making process. This book takes people step by step from evangelism to establishing new believers in the faith, equipping them in spiritual disciplines and gifts, and sending them out to engage the world with the gospel.

ESSENTIAL LEADERSHIP LESSONS
Richard J. Gehman
Essential Leadership Lessons covers topics of leadership essentials, humility, love, holiness, attributes, management skills, and common issues. While the context and application of these leadership lessons were created with the people of Africa in mind, the principles of Christian leadership are the same everywhere, for everyone, on all continents.

STAND UP FOR THE GOSPEL
Emmanuel Kwasi Amoafo
This book is a timely wake-up call about what is happening in many of our churches today. It will equip you to defend our timeless faith. In the midst of counterfeits, rediscover the refreshing truths of God's Word, and the glorious, life-transforming gospel of Jesus Christ.

I ONCE WAS DEAD
Cedric Kanana with Benjamin Fischer
This book's riveting, action-packed plot has one central message shining through: Jesus is stronger than death, than addiction, than Islam, than traditional religion, than curses. Trust Jesus alone! The miracles recorded in *I Once Was Dead* echo the book of Acts and give all glory to God – whether healing, deliverance, resurrection, protection from threats, or hearing God's voice.

THE ESSENTIAL GUIDE TO THE BIBLE AND CHRISTIANITY
John Jusu and Matthew Elliott
Situating each book of the Bible in the context the whole Bible clarifies truths that are less clear when taken out of context. This guide will help you understand, from a biblical perspective, how the visible world connects with the realities of the unseen world surrounding us.

THE SISTERHOOD SECRET
Levina Mulandi
In this book, Dr Mulandi shows how discipling is more than Bible study or a church program. She shares how she empowers any woman to mentor younger women, guiding them to understand their identity, discern the purpose of their lives, and be transformed to be more like Christ.

HAPPILY WHENEVER AFTER
Bookie Adekanye
Candid and kind, Bookie Adekanye reminds you of God's overwhelming love for you. No matter how society labels you, God says you belong to him. You're invited to heal from past scars and be your confident, courageous self. The God of the Bible used single ladies to deliver and save, and he definitely has a plan for you.

BAESICS
Ernest Wamboye with Waturi Wamboye
In *Baesics*, Ernest and Waturi Wamboye give no-nonsense advice on how to build a fulfilling love life and marriage. Young adults in African cities feel marriage is priority but are often unprepared. *Baesics* addresses the relationship dilemmas many young adults are facing today from a Christian point of view.

GETTING MARRIED?
Chao Tsuma Wanje and James Wanje
Written as a friendly and light-hearted conversation, this book is perfect for you and your fiancé(e) to read and discuss together. Drawing from timeless wisdom and real-life examples, this husband-and-wife team helps couples to resolve conflicts before they explode.

THE DIVORCE DILEMMA
Ron Misiko & Ray Motsi
The authors share their experiences as pastors and as married people, well as their areas of expertise in the legal system and Bible scholarship. From their different African context they explain how to navigate the challenges we face today with biblical and practical solutions for divorce in African churches.

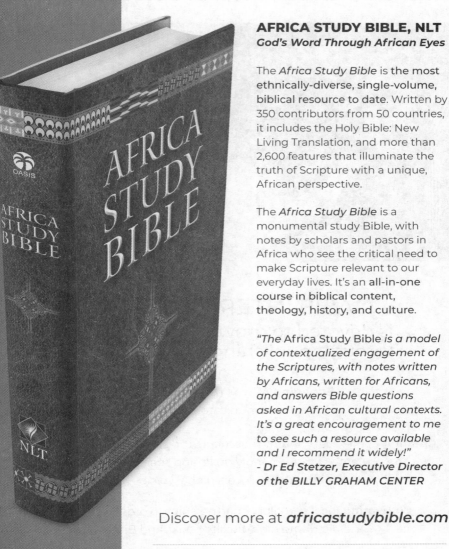

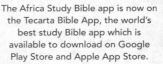

SATISFYING AFRICA'S THIRST FOR GOD'S WORD

OASIS INTERNATIONAL
is devoted to growing discipleship through publishing African voices.

Engaging Africa's most influential,
most relevant, and best communicators for the sake of the gospel.

Creating contextual content that meets the specific needs of Africa,
has the power to transform individuals and societies, and gives the
church in Africa a global voice.

Cultivating local and global partnerships in order to publish
and distribute high-quality books and Bibles.

Visit **oasisinternational.com** to learn more about our vision,
for Africa to equip its own leaders to impact the global church.